8) • Do the dead burn if they are set on fire? (Anonymo?) • Is paradise real? (Eliana, 7) • If you could choose, how would you die? (Yarmin, 7) • W[...] die at once? (Ariadna, 6) • Is paradise real? (Eliana, 8) • Can th[...] them? (Anonymous, 9) • Can a rabbit go to heaven? (Jana, 7) • [...] dead? (Mencía, 8) • How long does it take for our body to dec[...] • How can I live in peace if I know that I'm going to die? (Anony[...] women go up to heaven without wings? (Sira, 6) • How do mosquitoes die? (Clàudia, 5) • Do the plants that die in floods know they are dying? Do they feel any pain? (Gael, 7) • What happens if you go to hell and then come back to life? (Anonymous, 9) • Two questions for a vampire—do you have any blood in your body? How old are you? (Isabella, 5) • When you die, does your thinking stop? (Isaí, 5) • Are Death and the devil in cahoots? (Anonymous, 10) • When someone says, "I'm starving to death," are they really dying? (Sebastián, 5) • Where do you go when you are killed in an accident? (Anonymous, 10) • Can a dead person have fun? What does a dead person do for fun? (Elena, 5) • Is it reasonable for politicians and people to think euthanasia is bad without taking into consideration how much the person is suffering? (Mateo, 11) • What would you do if you were immortal? (Joana, 10) • Are we sure that at night we don't die and then come back to life in the morning? (Anonymous, 10) • How do we know that a dead person is really dead? (Eliana, 8) • How many times can a dead person visit their family? (Isabella, 5) • A question for a skeleton—how can you move if you don't have any muscles? (Florrie, 11) • When you die, do you remember everything? (Anonymous, 8) • Why do they put a picture outside (on the headstone)? (Sira, 6) • When you die, do you miss your body? (Yuma, 11) • If heaven and hell exist, is it possible to move back and forth from one to the other? (Guillermo, 15) • In the world of the dead, do people have emotions? (Aylin, 8) • Can you die from love or laughter? (Anonymous, 9) • Are there any animals in the world of the dead? (Sofía Eliana, 5) • A question for a vampire—would you like to die? (María Cecilia, 9) • If you are dead, can you think? (Anonymous, 9) • How do they make tombstones? (Sira, 6) • Does a skull ever get hungry? If it does, what does it eat? (Isabella, 5) • When we go up to heaven, does all our body go up? (Clàudia, 5) • Can you poop when you are dead? (Anonymous, 8) • With animals, is it the same as with people but without flowers? (Sira, 6) • How can we achieve absolute happiness in life? (Luz Mary, 13) • Where does a body take longer to decompose, in a graveyard or in a mausoleum? (Miguel Ángel, 13) • When you go to heaven, do you start a new life? (Anonymous, 9) • A question for a vampire—did you ever think you were going to die? (María Cecilia, 9) • If I die, who will get to keep my game console? (Gael, 7) • Should we fear death? (Adrián, 13) • When a hospital's resources are scarce because of a pandemic, does it make sense for them to give priority to treating the younger people? (Mateo, 11) • If you die and they hurt your body in the real world, do you feel it in heaven? (Anonymous, 9) • Will we go to heaven or to hell? (Hugo, 13) • When you die, do you become invisible? (Sofía Eliana, 5) • A question for a skeleton—Miss Skull, if one of your teeth falls out, does it grow back? (Isabella, 5) • Can you die while you are talking? (Anonymous, 8) • Why must there be something after death? (Adrián, 13) • If we die, will we meet our relatives? (Hugo, 13) • Would you prefer to die and for people to remember you when you are dead or to stay alive but for nobody to ever know who you are? (Africa, 13) • In the future, will there be special machines that bring the dead back to life? (Núria, 11) • Do dead people have feelings? (Anonymous, 9) • Is it true

what they say, that we go to heaven or hell? (Alejandro, 12) · Is there anything about your life that you would like to change before you die? (Pamela, 12) · In heaven, do you keep getting older or do you stay the same age? (Anonymous, 8) · A question for a skeleton— would you like to have skin? (María Cecilia, 9) · Would you like to reincarnate as a cat or a rabbit? (Fernanda, 8) · What would you do if you knew when you were going to die? (Joana, 10) · When you are dead and underground, can you breathe? (Clàudia, 5) · Why do we have to die? (Fazeel, 8; Gael, 7, and Jóhann, 12) · Would you like to live someone else's life? (Joana, 10) · What would you do if you were going to die in an hour's time? (Tatiana, 11) · How long are you in heaven for? (Anonymous, 9) · What happens if when we die, we have issues pending or unresolved? (Uzinga, 11) · Can animals see ghosts? (Miguel Ángel, 13) · How can we be sure that we are going to be OK when we die? (Anonymous, 11) · Does hell exist? (Francisco, 7) · When you die, do people remember all the things you used to do with them? (Sira, 6) · Why isn't life forever? (Francisco, 7) · Do the dead die? If they don't die, where are they? (Anonymous, 11) · If a device's batteries have run out, is it dead? (Fausto, 5) · Why will everyone die some day? (Sofía Eliana, 5) · Is death alive or dead? (Mariana, 8) · Why do some people die at a younger age than others? (Olmo, 11) · How many times do you have to behave badly to be sent to hell? (Anonymous, 9) · If my parents die, is it true that they'll look after me from heaven? (Álex, 9) · Before I was born, where was I? Was I dead? (Maya, 9) · When you die, can you see death? (Vania, 8) · Can you eat when you are dead? (Sofía Eliana, 5) · When you die, do you meet up with your ancestors? (Anonymous, 9) · Is death with me, watching me? (Sara, 11) · Why do we use flowers to remember the dead? (Sira, 6) · When you die, your soul goes to heaven, but where is your soul when you are alive? (Anonymous, 11) · Will life on this planet last forever? (Ander, 11) · Does each person feel death differently? (Pablo, 11) · Does death die? (Juan, 11, and Mireia, 6) · Who takes care of the children when parents die? (Sofía Eliana, 5) · What am I going to do when I'm dead? (Anonymous, 9) · If death is with us from the moment we are born, when you die, does death stay by our side? (Tere, 10) · A question for a vampire—when you weren't immortal, were you afraid of dying? (Gael, 8) · Am I going to see my dead relatives when I die? (Anonymous, 9) · Is there anything you want to do before you die? (Pamela, 12) · Is death watching us? (Sara, 11) · Does the memory of vampires last as long as the memory of humans? (María Cecilia, 9) · Do the dead gradually become invisible? (Anonymous, 8) · When we faint, do we die for an instant? (Álex, 9) · If death is nothing, who is death? (Ander, 11) · Do the dead have fun? (Aylin, 8) · Do you think it's possible to resuscitate? (Guillermo, 15) · Would you like to be a vampire? (Fernanda, 8) · Is there an age limit? (Maily, 10, and Santi, 11) · How long are you sad for if you die? What about if your mother dies? (Anonymous, 10) · Why exactly do we die? (Marcos, 15) · When we die, are we aware at that exact moment in time of what is happening to us? (Isabel, 14) · What things bring meaning to your life? (Tatiana, 11) · If ghosts exist, what shape are they? (Anonymous, 8) · Would you like to be immortal? (Pamela, 12) · Why should we talk about death? (Anonymous, 11) · Is it possible to dream of the real feeling of death? Or is it a feeling that only manifests itself once? (Isabel, 14) · How can you tell that you will die soon? (Eloi, 11) · Can you die when you have only just been born? (Maily, 10) · Can the dead see? (Aylin, 8) · What happens with everything I have to do if I die before I was meant to die? (Anonymous, 11) · Do you think your life has as much meaning as a millionaire's life? (Tatiana, 11) ·

DYING TO ASK

38 QUESTIONS FROM KIDS ABOUT DEATH

For Iain
Ellen

For Clàudia and Gael
Anna

DYING TO ASK

38 QUESTIONS FROM KIDS ABOUT DEATH

ELLEN DUTHIE & ANNA JUAN CANTAVELLA, PH.D.
ILLUSTRATED BY ANDREA ANTINORI

T tra.publishing

Contents

About This Book

Dear mortal,

Thank you very much for choosing this book and congratulations on being brave enough to open it!

Death is a peculiar subject matter. We feel curious and intrigued by its mystery, but it can also be scary and unsettling. Have you ever covered your eyes in the middle of a scary movie? Have you then opened your fingers, slowly, to peek through the gaps, before quickly closing them tight again? Look at that finger choreography! You want to look, and you do not want to look; you want to know, and you do not want to know.

The wonderful thing about a book is that you can close it whenever you like. Bam! And you can then decide to open it a minute later because, in fact, on second thought, you do want to read a little more, or perhaps you want to try a different chapter. Or you might want to leave it closed until another day, another month, or another year, when you are more in the mood for a book about death.

But before experimenting with opening and closing these pages, we would like to tell you a bit about how this book came to exist.

Like most human beings, the writers of *Dying to Ask* (Anna and Ellen) find death fascinating, but also scary. Many human beings try to avoid thinking about death at all costs, hiding it away and very rarely discussing it. This is true among adults, but especially when it comes to their talking about death with children and young people. However, in our literature and philosophy workshops with children and teens, whenever the subject of death comes up, we have noticed how interested everybody is to explore questions and talk about issues regarding death freely and deeply. So, we set ourselves a challenge: Could we write a book that might spark the same kind of interesting and varied conversations about death as those that take place in our workshops? We thought so!

We knew from the start that we wanted to build the book around real questions from real mortals. So, we set to work.

We organized a series of workshops designed for thinking, imagining, and wondering about death. When we had perfected the workshops, we created a booklet *(DYING TO ASK! Vital Ideas for Sparking Mortal Questions)* for anyone to download for free, and invited families, schools, and libraries across the world to do these workshops and to take part in the project by sending us all their mortal questions.

We received hundreds of questions from different locations across the world (Spain, Italy, Finland, Germany, United Kingdom, United States, Colombia, Mexico, Argentina, Ecuador, Brazil, and Turkey).

Once we had gathered all the questions, it was time to sort them and choose. Can you imagine how hard that was?

Look at the Contents page to check out our final selection. You will see questions of all sorts: scientific, philosophical, anthropological, psychological, as well as very practical ones. You will also find funny and sad questions, hard and easy questions, uncomfortable, brave, surprising, and playful questions. The thirty-eight questions that are the titles of each of the chapters are a representative sample of the rich variety of interests, curiosities, and concerns about death voiced by the living beings between the ages of 5 and 15 who took part in the project.

Before or after reading this book, you can also download...
... the question-provoking booklet *DYING TO ASK! Vital Ideas for Sparking Mortal Questions*. Enjoy!
trapublishing.com/pages/resources

Once we had chosen the questions, along came the illustrator (Andrea) with a mission. Without reading any of the answers to the questions, he set out to give his own kind of interpretation and reaction to each of them, through his drawings. So, one way of reading the illustrations in this book is to think of them as answers or playful explorations of the questions.

Then, with all the drawings finished, we wrote the final versions of our answers. We particularly enjoyed being able to play and interact not only with the questions but also with Andrea's illustrations.

It has been a truly fascinating and fun book to create. In fact, it was so much fun and so fascinating that it took us three years to finish it. Three years! We knew it would take a while, but we now have irrefutable proof that you simply cannot answer questions about death in a hurry. Most questions about death don't have a satisfying, straightforward answer. We had to dive in and explore different possible ways of answering and thinking about things. The answers you will find in this book are the accounts of our particular explorations.

What we would really like is for these exploratory answers to bring about good conversations, and many more questions. Questions never die.

Long live questions!

When to Read This Book

We generally only read or think about death when a loved one dies or when death touches us in some other way. We can read this book at those times if we wish, but it is not a book created specifically for times of grief.

It is an invitation to think and talk about death naturally, at any time, and from many different points of view.

In other words, you can read it whenever you like!

How to Read This Book

You can read this book alone or with others, but even if you read it alone first, you are likely to want to talk about it with other people, because that is what tends to happen with all things mortal. You want to share them.

You can read it from start to finish, one answer after the other. Or you can skip, jump, and go back and forth, as you like, letting your curiosity, your interest or your fear (boo!) be your guide.

(You will also find suggestions for chapters to jump to at the end of each answer).

Another way of reading this book is thinking of your own questions as you read it and writing them down somewhere special or sharing them with anyone you like.

Each of the chapters contain details, stories, or pieces of information you might want to know more about. You can make your own inquiries and complete each answer with other information, ideas, or readings that you look for yourself.

In other words, you can read it however you like!

This book...
... contains questions by mortals from various parts of the world, but not from every part. It is likely, or at the very least possible, that this book might be quite different if it contained questions from other areas of the world.

Dying to Ask...
... deals primarily with the death of human beings. Many other kinds of beings die every day. That would make for another fascinating book, or several.

Our most enthusiastic thanks...
... to all the lovely mortals between the ages of 5 and 15 who took part in the project and came up with the intriguing questions in this book that will spark interesting conversations among its readers. Thank you!

1. Will I die?

Clàudia

IS THERE ANY WAY OF ESCAPING DEATH?

Dear Clàudia,

Lucky you! Yours is one of the few questions about death that has a perfectly simple and straightforward answer. In one word: yes.

But even though "yes" is the exact right answer, don't you think it feels a bit too short?

Certain questions deserve more than the right answer. So, let us say a little more.

The statement "I will die" is as true as this other one: "$2 + 2 = 4$." In other words, there is no way of escaping death. If you are a human being, you will die. You can say it loud and clear, with no fear of making a mistake or lying. I WILL DIE!

But don't worry, Clàudia. You are not alone! When it comes to mortality, you have plenty of company. Sooner or later, death arrives for all human beings. One day (hopefully in a reasonably distant future) the writers and the illustrator of this book will die, and so will our families, our friends, our pets, and our plants. We are mortal.

What if...
... instead of a human being, you were an immortal jellyfish (*Turritopsis dohrnii*)? Well, you may manage to escape the claws of death, but it is very unlikely that you could ever read this book.

What is particularly difficult for us humans (and not so difficult for our pets or our plants) is that not only are we mortal, but we know it!

The first time you think of your own mortality, the idea might feel scary. The second and third time it may well have the same effect. Shudder!

When you think of a question like "Will I die?" sometimes, if you scratch a little, you might reveal other questions or concerns underneath that, which are more difficult to answer:

Might I die soon?

Will it hurt or will it not hurt?

What will it feel like to be dead?

It feels strange and unsettling to know in such certain terms that something will occur, but not to have the faintest idea of when it will take place, how it will happen, or what it will feel like.

The uncertainty is unbearable! On the one hand, we might be tempted to cover our eyes and ears and never ever think about death again. We are scared. On the other hand, we are probably dying to know more. We are curious.

Home experiment
Close your eyes and try to imagine the feeling of not being alive.
Do you think it might be impossible?

But think about it. Would you really want to know more? How much more would you want to know? And what would you do with the information? There are no easy answers.

So, what can we do with all these questions about death that pop up in our minds every now and then, some of them without answers?

Here is a suggestion: one of the most comforting things we can do with our own mortality and our questions about death is to share them with other mortal beings. This way, the twenty-fourth time we think of our own mortality, we might find the idea slightly more normal and just a little bit less scary.

PS What a great question to open the book with, Clàudia!

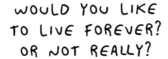

WOULD YOU LIKE TO LIVE FOREVER? OR NOT REALLY?

Mortal knowledge questionnaire
Would you like to know the exact date of your own death? Why? What advantages and what disadvantages would there be in knowing the date? Would you live your life differently if you knew you were going to live a short life? What about if you knew with absolute certainty that you were going to live a very, very long life?

You might also be interested in questions 9 and 37.

2. How does skin go away?

Nacho

Dear Nacho,

What an elegant way of asking about skeletonization!

Let us start politely, with a greeting. Look at your body, all covered in skin. Take one of your arms and touch it. Feel the skin and the flesh underneath. Press down gently to feel your bones. Now touch one of your cheeks. Does it feel nice and bouncy? Yes, but feel for the bones nearby, the cheekbone above, the jaw below. Move up and touch the skin around one of your eyes and feel the socket in your skull. Hello, skeleton!

Skeletons are very familiar to us, and not only through touch. They are everywhere: in movies, stories, museums, and festivities. They operate as a symbol: as soon as we see them, we understand that they represent death. But it is one thing to think of those skeletons and another quite different thing to think of *your own skeleton*. Visualizing ourselves as skeletons reminds us that we are mortal. Oh, woe!

But let's shake off those spine chills and cut to the chase.

Unless we choose to be cremated after we die, it is highly likely that, one day, all that will be left of our body is our skeleton. And another day will come, in the yet more distant future, when even our bones will be gone. Puff! Bye-bye, body. But how? How does flesh disappear? How does skin go away?

Can you imagine watching a body from the moment it dies until there is nothing left but bones? It would take a while (weeks, months, maybe years!), and it might not be the most pleasant experience, but it would certainly be fascinating.

The heart has stopped. The body's cells start breaking down. As they break down, they begin to release gases and other substances that smell awful to human beings but announce a banquet to other living beings along the food chain. The first to arrive are the bacteria that were already in the body, led by those that were hanging about the intestines, which start reproducing quickly and spreading. Almost immediately the insects arrive (flies are particularly speedy). And finally, the worms (the larvae of those insects) join in too, together with other bacteria, fungi and microorganisms that come from outside. They all gradually make their way through the soft parts of the body. The process of putrefaction is under way. It happens little by little and in different overlapping phases.

Variable speed
A corpse that is out in the open decomposes twice as fast as a corpse in water and eight times faster than a corpse underground. A corpse in a coffin or in a niche grave also takes longer to become a skeleton. This is because the insects involved in the decomposition of bodies have easier access to the corpse if it is in the open or on the ground.

What about the bones?
Bones take much longer to disappear. A skeleton can last anywhere between twenty and thousands of years!

The body's internal organs start to liquefy first, little by little, before "vanishing"—the liver, the spleen, the intestines, the heart... until there is nothing left of them.

In the meantime, the skin has started to dry up and crack, and comes away bit by bit. With the skin, off come the nails, the hair... until there is nothing left but the skeleton!

This process can last anywhere between a few weeks to a few years. In areas where it is hot and humid, a body can become a skeleton in just two weeks. In areas where it is freezing and the air is very dry, however, the bacteria and the bugs find it harder to sink their teeth in (in a manner of speaking) and the putrefaction process is slower. Sometimes, it can even come to a halt altogether. In these cases, the skin comes off, but rather than drying up, it sticks to the bones and stays there. What do you think we call skeletons with skin that never went away? Yup, mummies!

And so, the time has come to say goodbye. Not all bodies turn into skeletons. If someone chooses to be cremated, their body does not even have time to decompose, let alone become a skeleton! Also, the cremation temperature is so high that not even the bones remain. What is left is ashes. Bye-bye, skeleton!

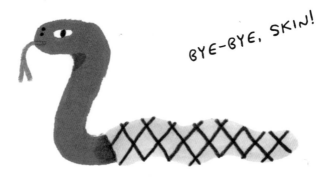

BYE-BYE, SKIN!

You might also be interested in questions 4, 17, and 36.

3. When you die, does your thinking stop?

Isaí

Dear Isaí,

Your question is a good one, and like most good questions,
it happens to be an incredibly old one too.

Science tells us that there are two types of death: clinical death
(when the heartbeat, blood circulation, and breathing stops); and
biological death, also known as brain death (when the brain stops
receiving oxygen and no longer has any activity). Normally, brain
death takes place a few minutes after clinical death. And just then,
yes, we could say that our thinking stops.

But with questions about death, scientific answers are not always
fully satisfying, are they? In this case, many other questions remain.
The body dies, yes, but aren't human beings more than just a body?
You can touch your body, but not your thoughts. Is your brain the
same thing as your mind? What about everything we cannot touch
but still feels part of us? Could it be that some of what we cannot
touch might somehow stay around after we die?

It is true that it is impossible to answer these questions with any
certainty (no dead person has ever come back to let us know
whether they are still thinking or not!). But thankfully we can
always resort to imagination.

What do you think?
Does our thinking stop when we die? And if it does not stop, how
does it all work? What does your imagination tell you? And what do
people around you think? Try conducting a survey. When we die,
does our thinking stop? Or not?

And who do you think...
... will win the game? The skeleton or the half-bodied man? Why?

You might also be interested in questions 4, 5, 32, and 36.

4. When we die, does all our body die at once?

Ariadna

Dear Ariadna,

Some questions about death are funny, others are scary, and others spark curiosity. Yours manages to do all these things at once: it is comical, it is unnerving, and it is altogether fascinating to think about. What a question!

As you can see for yourself, the illustrator thought it would be fun to play with the comical side of your question. Look at Queen Marie Antoinette's head skateboarding away from the guillotine, determined to survive a little longer than her body. Where is her head heading? To change history? Or to enjoy her favorite worldly pleasure for the very last time? And what's your bet? Will death get there before the executioner?

When we (the writers) read your question, we also thought it was amusing. The idea of living body parts coexisting with dead body parts seemed like a great premise for a joke.

But when we set to work, instead of a joke, all we got was an unsettling question. If our body does not die all at once, would there be a time when we were half dead or half alive? Eek! What is concerning about this idea is the possibility that the living part of our body might be aware of everything and might feel pain, suffering or simply dismay at the realization that the other half is dead. Let's face it, if we could choose, most of us would probably prefer all our body to die at once. Bam! And that's that.

However, we're sorry to break it to you and everyone else who is reading this book—that's not that. Bodies never die all at once. Even when death is sudden, like in an accident, death is always a process. When the heart stops, the blood stops circulating, and the oxygen can no longer reach the cells of the various parts and organs of the body. Cells with the highest oxygen requirements are the first to die; whereas cells that can operate with less oxygen survive a little longer.

But here comes the good news, Ariadna! Brain cells need a lot of oxygen to survive, so they don't last long at all without it. They die straight away. Thank goodness! From that moment onwards, even though we are in the process of dying, little by little, we aren't aware of anything.

Around an hour later, the cells of the heart, the pancreas, the liver and the kidneys will have died. The cells of the skin and the corneas of our eyes can stay alive up to a few hours, but our white blood cells can survive up to two to three days after our heart has stopped.

So no, our body does not die all at once. And yes, there will be some parts that are still alive while others have already died. But Queen Marie Antoinette's head would not be able to enjoy that last drink, because her brain would be dead, and a dead brain can no longer enjoy anything (woe!), nor can it suffer (phew!).

SLURP!

You might also be interested in questions 2, 3, 5, and 36.

Have you ever stopped to think that...
... thanks to the fact that our bodies do not die all at once,
we can transplant body organs that are still alive to the bodies
of people who need them, and save their lives?

5. How do we know that a dead person is really dead?

Eliana

Dear Eliana,

Can you imagine waking up inside a coffin underground? Aaaaaaah! Help!

But, shhh! You don't want to shout. You really don't. Oxygen is in short supply, and you need to make it last. Breathe as slowly and as deeply as you can, and wish, pray, and hope, with all your heart, that someone comes to open your tomb and saves you before it's too late, and you end up dying for real.

There! You can now wake up from that nightmare! *Taphophobia* is the fear of being buried alive by mistake. It may seem a little far-fetched now, because in the 21st century the chances of something like this happening to us are slim to nonexistent. But this was not always the case.

A long time ago, doctors didn't have the kind of tools and instruments available today to help them determine whether a patient was indeed dead or not quite. All they had at their disposal was their senses (especially hearing, touch, and sight). If the heart stopped beating (they could no longer feel the person's pulse) and if there were no external signs of breathing (the person's chest wasn't visibly moving up and down and no air could be felt coming out of their mouth or nose), then the person was pronounced dead. Sometimes, it is true, it was hard to tell whether someone had actually died, or if it only seemed like they had died. Frighteningly often, these doubts ended in tragedies or situations like the one depicted in the illustration (OK, minus the phone): "Hey! I'm still alive!"

Are you ready for a real-life example? On a rainy autumn day in 1571, in the English village of Braughing, the bearers of a coffin of one Mathew Wall slipped on the carpet of wet leaves covering the lane to the cemetery. Picture the thump and the crash. Down they all went, followed by the coffin. Inside, young Mathew woke up from the commotion and started banging on the lid –bam! bam! bam!– for someone to open it up. Out he came, alive and kicking, and went on to live for many more years.

Mathew was lucky, but there were many other cases where, by the time it was discovered that a body had been buried by mistake, it was too late. When they opened the coffin, the person inside had ended up dying after all.

These tragic errors gave rise to the habit of waiting for a few days before burying a dead body (to ensure they did not wake up, and that decomposition was already underway). Some people left a written note in their will requesting that their heart be pierced with a needle to make sure they were not buried alive. Thankfully, the invention of the stethoscope in the 19th century put an end to the need for all that heart piercing. Phew!

But even though medical advances like the stethoscope helped reduce the possibility of making mistakes, the way of determining whether a person was really dead remained the same. However, with the arrival of other medical advances, such as the mechanical ventilator or artificial respirator, and the possibility of performing heart transplants, it became clear that it was no longer enough to detect an absence of breathing and an absence of heartbeat to pronounce someone dead —after all, both of these things could be true and yet the patient might not be irreversibly dead. A new way of diagnosing death was called for.

How about...
... a "safety coffin"? In the 19th century several models were patented, equipped with flags, breathing tubes, bells and all sorts of contraptions that could be activated from the inside to warn people on the outside that the person in there was not dead, but alive and kicking.

In the mid-20th century, several medical studies led to the distinction between *clinical death* (when the heartbeat stops and the breathing ceases), which can still sometimes be reversed, and *brain death* (when the brain stops working, making it impossible for the breathing and the pulse to return). Since then, there has been a lot of medical research into death, and there are now instruments and tests, such as electroencephalograms, that are capable of detecting when the brain stops working and death is irreversible. So today it is much easier to tell an apparent death from an irreversible death, and it is close to impossible for someone to be buried alive.

AND HOW DO WE KNOW THAT A LIVING PERSON IS REALLY ALIVE?

You may also be interested in questions 3, 4, 30, and 32.

6. How do we die?

Leo

Dear Leo,

Human beings die in (almost) every way you might imagine.

Including the unfortunate way the man in the illustration is about to die? It is a very unusual way to die, but there have been a few cases of pianos falling on people and causing their death, yes. In the year 1903, in the Spanish city of Logroño, a man called Cipriano García lost his life when a black grand piano they were hoisting through the window of a building gave way and fell on top of him. But you probably shouldn't worry too much about it, because in a ranking of possible ways of dying, being flattened by a black grand piano would be right down at the bottom, possibly just above being flattened by a pink grand piano.

And what way of dying would top the ranking? In the 21st century, human beings die from heart disease more than any other cause.

Of course, you may well have asked your question not so much out of an interest in statistics as out of some kind of concern. What way of dying is the most painful? How about the least painful? Are some ways of dying more dignified than others? To share another of the questions we received for this book: "If I die making a silly face, will it stay like that forever?"

If you could decide how to die, what would you prefer? A sudden, quick death (where you didn't even notice it, even if this meant that you could not say goodbye to your loved ones) or a slower, more anticipated death (where you were aware that you were dying, and had enough time to say goodbye)? Why?

Is it possible for someone to laugh to death?
It's unlikely but not impossible. The Greek philosopher Chrysippus saw a donkey eating some figs, found it absolutely hilarious, and cried out "Now give the donkey a drink of wine to wash down the figs." He was then so overcome with amusement by his own utterance that he started laughing to the point of choking to death. And the moral of the story is—don't laugh at your own jokes!

You might also be interested in questions 19, 27, and 29.

7. When do

we die?

Zeno

Dear Zeno,

Humans can die at many different moments, but it is true that some moments to die are more usual than others. For instance, if someone died at the age of 80 or 90, nobody would think that it was either an extraordinarily young or a surprisingly old age to die. But some people don't die until well after their one hundredth birthday! And even though more people today live long lives than ever before, human beings can die in youth or in childhood, right after they are born, or even before they are born. Strictly speaking, we can die any time.

Any time? Eek! The very idea that death could strike us right here and now as we read these words is troubling, to say the least. We may feel tempted to look around in search for clues. We might glance at the clock, as if it could tell us how long we have left. Those seconds go by so, so slowly. In any case, it would take altogether too long to try to count the seconds until our death. A whole lifetime!

Even though the idea that we could die at any moment may be unsettling, it could also drive and inspire us in ways that are interesting. If we could die at any moment, let's make the most of every single instant, just in case it is our last!

As the Latin saying goes, *carpe diem!* ("seize the day!"). And as you say in English (most languages have some version of the same expression): "life is short!"

What about our friend the immortal jellyfish? Does it never die? Of course it dies! Even though it sounds paradoxical, biologically immortal organisms are certainly mortal. It may be that these jellyfish escape death from old age but there's no escaping other fatal dangers such as predators, diseases, or catastrophic climate changes. Our friend, much like us, can die at any time. Eek! Carpe diem to you too, jellyfish!

But is a lifespan of 80 or 90 years really that short? It all depends on who or what we compare ourselves with. Some animals and plants die shortly after they are born, and others die following a very, very, very, long life. A human being has an incredibly lengthy life if we compare it to the life of a mayfly, for example (an adult mayfly lives about 24 hours if lucky). Male ants don't tend to live much longer than three weeks. Flies have only 15 to 30 days to do everything they'd like to do in life. If all goes well, a fieldmouse might live to the ripe old age of 18 months. A wolf might make it all the way to age nine, which is not much compared to pet dogs and cats, whose sheltered lives can afford them a 17th birthday party. What about an African elephant? It can live to the age of about 70, almost as long as a human.

Of course, 70 years is hardly a big deal compared with the life of an Aldabra giant tortoise (up to 183 years), a bowhead whale (200 years), or a Greenland shark (300 years). What a life! Yes, but again, that's nothing compared with a particular type of clam living off the coast of Iceland, with a potential lifespan of up to 500 years. That's five centuries. Half a millennium! And we haven't even got started with plants! There's a South American cushion plant known as *yareta*, with specimens that have been around for 3,000 years. Some bristlecone pines are known to have been with us for 5,000 years, and then we have the *Jōmon Sugi*, a cryptomeria tree on the Japanese island of Yakushima. It has been on planet Earth for seven millennia —and counting! How's that for a lifetime?

WHEN WILL
I DIE?

You might also be interested in questions 8 and 35.

8. Is there an age limit?

Maily

NOT TODAY, THANK YOU VERY MUCH!

Dear Maily,

On the date we are writing this letter, the oldest living person in the world is US born Spanish citizen Maria Branyas Morera. She is... (drumroll)... 117 years old! Impressive? Well, wait for it. Jeanne Calment was a French woman who died in 1997, at the oldest age anyone has ever been known to die. She lived no less than 122 years and 164 days. Can you imagine getting to celebrate your 122nd birthday? Can you picture it?

Your question makes us wonder. If we can live to the age of 122, could we live to the age of 123? Or 124? What about 150? 200? 500? 1,000? No, not 1,000. And not 500 either. Not even 200. Although there is no agreement as to the exact age limit for humans, few scientists hold that we will ever be able to live more than 150 years (and many others believe that Jeanne Calment's 122 years might be just about the limit).

But what is it that makes 150 years the limit and not 200, for instance? Part of the reason for that precise limit lies in our cells. During our lives, our cells die and are replaced all the time. They die at a rate of one million per second (per second!) and they are replaced thanks to the neat trick of cell division. One cell can become two. Not bad! But there is a trick to this "trick": it can only be resorted to a certain number of times. After that, cells start to behave erratically. Besides this "factory defect," cells also deteriorate due to other factors. When we are young and healthy, our body manages to repair cells with relative ease, but after certain illnesses, and with every birthday that goes by, it takes more work and more time to complete the process of renovation and repair. By the time we are 120 years old, our body can hardly repair cells at all. This is when the body dies. And there you have your age limit.

You might be interested in questions 7, 9, 35, and 37.

A question for you.
What do you think would be the perfect age limit? Why?

9. Why do we have to die?

Fazeel

WHAT WOULD
HAPPEN
IF NO ONE
EVER DIED?

Dear Fazeel,

You may have asked your question out of scientific curiosity ("Why do we die?"). If this is what you are interested in, don't forget to read the previous question in this book, sent to us by Maily ("Is there an age limit?"), which is interestingly related to yours.

But the way you phrased your question made us think it might be more of a lament. "Oh! Why, oh why do we have to die? Is it really absolutely necessary for us to die?" Believe us, we understand. It is hard to live with the idea that, someday, we will die!

Why don't we try something? Imagine the opposite was true. Imagine we didn't have to die. Eternal life on Earth for us all! Coming right up!

Let us take this game seriously and try to imagine this death-free life in detail. If we didn't die, would we grow older? Forever older and older? In which case, what would we look like and what would our quality of life be at the age of 350? What about at the age of 1,000? Or would we stop aging at some point? At what age might that happen? Let us keep playing. If aging were to stop at some point, what would be the perfect age for us to stop aging and live forever after?

Another question...
... we received for this book is similar, but it makes us think of slightly different answers: "Is it important to die?"

Just a moment! If nobody ever died, you could have a baby sharing a house with a person who might be two or three thousand years old! Can you imagine living with your great great great great great great grandmother? How old would she be now? Do you think the world would be a more interesting place if people from the past and the present all lived together? Can you envision any complications? What would we spend our eternities doing? Do you think we might eventually become bored of our eternal life? And what would planet Earth look like? Can you think of a way of providing enough space for so many people? If you could make this eternal life on Earth a reality by clicking your fingers, would you?

Can you imagine how incredibly different life would be if there was no death? Wait! Would we even call it "life" if there was no death?

You might also be interested in questions 1, 8, 15, and 37.

10. Who takes care of the children when parents die?

Sofía Eliana

Dear Sofía Eliana,

Most of us have wondered about your question at some point, perhaps out of worry or simply out of curiosity. Like lots of the other questions in this book, this one has many different possible answers. Exactly what would happen to us if we became orphans depends on many different things.

For example, in cases where someone dies after a long illness, where they know beforehand that they are going to die, there may be time to do some planning and think carefully about who they would like to choose as their children's new legal guardians after their death.

They may even have time to talk about it with their kids and with the person or people chosen, to make sure they would be happy to take on such an important role. If everyone agrees, the name of the person or people chosen as legal guardians is then set out in a document called the Last Will and Testament.

When there is enough time to plan and to draw up legal documents, it makes things easier because the wishes of everyone involved are clearly stated.

What do books and movies tell us?

Has it ever struck you that there are many, many, many books and movies with orphans as main characters? If we take a closer look at who takes care of some of these famous fictional orphans, it's no wonder we might feel concerned. Take Harry Potter, with his gruesome aunt, horrendous uncle, and ghastly cousin. Or Cinderella, with that cruel stepmother and those vile stepsisters. Then we have the Baudelaire kids, from *A Series of Unfortunate Events*, passed around from relative to relative, each worse than the last. At least they have interesting adventures! But then we also have Pippi Longstocking, who has the pleasure of living alone and doing whatever she likes. Whoopee! But might that be more fun to read about in a book or watch in a film than to experience it in real life? It's a good job that fiction is just that—fiction!

However, in the case of more sudden deaths (like in an accident, for example) it may be that no legal guardians have been appointed and that no conversation has ever been had about who would take care of the children in the event of the death of the parents.

In this case, what tends to happen is that a relative requests legal guardianship of the children. If there are several family members or people who wish to be the children's guardians, a decision is made taking into consideration the children's best interests.

Once a guardian or guardians are appointed, they are entrusted with the care, support, and love of the child until they are of legal age (and beyond!).

Although it's not so common, it does sometimes happen that there are no relatives or people close to the family who can become the child or children's legal guardians. In these cases, the children normally go and live in a foster home, where they are looked after until a legal guardian can be appointed or until they are of legal age.

And in case you are wondering, no! Pets cannot be appointed as legal guardians. But don't you think it would make a great idea for a book or a movie?

TEETH!

You might also be interested in reading questions 14 and 18.

11. What is there after death?

Hugo

Dear Hugo,

Your question shines a light on what is very likely to be the most mysterious of all of life's mysteries. Which is saying a lot, because if there's anything this life is not lacking, that's mystery!

Human beings have been asking themselves your question since forever. Ever since we have existed. What is there after death? What might there be?

And can you believe that, after thousands of years of wondering about your question and coming up with all kinds of possibilities, we are as far from reaching a final answer as we were when we started? Some questions are just like that!

But what does the science say? If we look at things from a strictly scientific view, there is no proof that there is anything after death or anything beyond our biological organism. The answer to your question would be, according to the evidence available—nothing. After death, there is nothing.

It is true that the remains of all dead organisms serve as nutrients for other living beings. We could say that, in a way, nature recycles us. So, the answer to your question could also be—recycling. After death, there is recycling.

Some people believe that human beings are just a body (and that our self cannot live on, once our body dies). If you are one of these people, perhaps "nothing" or "recycling" will feel like more or less satisfactory answers to your question. When our body dies, we cease to exist. And that's that!

But even people who believe we are all body, sometimes find it hard to imagine "nothing." Here is another question we received for this book: 'When I ask myself "what is there after death?", my answer is 'nothing.' But I then wonder—"What is 'nothing'?"

It's hard to imagine death as an absolute end! How can it be that when we die everything that we are disappears forever? Might there not be a part of us that doesn't die and goes on "living" in another world, in a different way?

Throughout history, human beings have sought answers to your question by looking beyond science. In fact, religions arise to try to provide answers to questions like yours.

In most religions, each in its own way, there is a belief that, in addition to our body, human beings have souls. And when the body dies and decomposes, the soul remains somehow—it is immortal.

We normally imagine this immortal part of us as ethereal, without color, density, or shape. As something that floats and can fly to that Great Beyond where the souls of the dead people go.

This belief in a soul and in a life after death is almost as old as your question. What varies is the way every different religion imagines the soul. But that is a whole different story... (turn the page).

You might also be interested in questions 12 and 13.

What do you think?
When we die, will we be welcomed to the world of the dead with a festive greeting, or will it be an altogether more solemn occasion? Will we reincarnate and live a different life? Will we hang around Earth in the form of spirits or ghosts? Or is being remembered by those who once knew us the only way we will live on, in some way?

12. Where do we go when we die?

Manuela

Dear Manuela,

Your question makes a perfect pair with Hugo's (question number 11). If you haven't already read his chapter, you may want to read that first. If you go back to page 48, we'll wait for you here. Did you read it? Great. On we go, then.

If you don't believe in souls and are persuaded that when our body dies, everything we are dies with it, the answer to your question would be this—when we die, we don't go anywhere. We simply cease to exist. Bye-bye!

We could of course choose to focus on the body. Where does the body of a deceased person go when it dies? From the hospital to the funeral home, and from the funeral home to the cemetery, perhaps. Or from the person's house to the funeral home and from the funeral home to the crematorium. Could be. We could also suggest, if the deceased person happened to be an organ donor, that some of their body parts (a kidney or their heart, for example) might "go" to other bodies and go on living in them.

However, if you believe we have a soul or some other thing that survives death, you are probably not particularly interested in hearing about where bodies or organs go. As soon as we think of the possibility of a life after death, we are interested to know all the details. Where will this life take place? What will it be like? Will I like it? In that life, will I meet up with my dead relatives? And will I be able to chat with them, like when they were alive?

In addition to your question and Hugo's, many of the other questions we received for this book share your curiosity. Some express concern: "How can we be sure that we will be OK when we die?" Others delve into the logic of it all: "Do we celebrate birthdays when we are dead?" And if we do celebrate birthdays, do we celebrate the day of our birth or the day of our death? Other questions are more practical: "What am I going to do when I'm dead?", "When you die, do you still go to school (even if nobody can see you)?"

What if we don't go anywhere at all when we die and simply hang around planet Earth in the form of ghosts or spirits? Oh, no! Can you imagine an afterlife that was just... rather boring?

No way! The afterlives described in most religions are generally anything but boring! We find tales of underworlds and paradises where souls go after bodies die. Bright heavens beyond hanging bridges, and lush gardens with milk and honey streams and golden palaces. Terrifying underground hells with wells of souls, dungeons, rivers of flame, dark and desolate plains, and labyrinthine cells. And all those places halfway between the underworld and paradise: purgatories, limbos, edgeless spaces and endless meadows to walk through for all of eternity. Places inhabited by gods, archangels , demons, three headed dogs, and other supernatural creatures.

In religions such as Christianity or Islam, what determines where someone's soul goes after death is how the deceased person led their life. If they lived in accordance with their religion's norms, paradise awaits them. If, on the other hand, they disobeyed any of the rules of their religion or lived as an unbeliever, then gloomy, dark, and bad places could be in store for them.

For the Aztecs and the Vikings, on the other hand, the place you went to after death was not so much marked by the life you had led, but by the manner and circumstances in which you died. For instance, if you died in battle you would go to a different place than if you were struck by lightning, drowned, or died from old age.

What about reincarnation? Is it possible that where our soul goes when we die is to a different body? An infinite cycle of death and rebirth! Sounds fun, doesn't it? "I want to be a cat!" "Could I be a giraffe now, please?" But let's not get too excited. That's not exactly how it's meant to work. Hinduism believers, for instance, hold that souls reincarnate, but that they do not remember their past existences. So, it would be a cycle of death and rebirth into other bodies and forms, but with no memory of previous lives. Does that seem less fun? Maybe, but maybe not!

Who knows? Since nobody who has died has come back to tell the tale, it is impossible to answer your question with any certainty. But if you had to imagine an afterlife in detail, how would you picture it? Would we reach it by escalator, through holes in the ground, or across hanging bridges? What different places would there be in your afterlife? Would it be inhabited by supernatural beings, or would it be a more homey place, where we could spend our time playing cards, reading good books, and laughing at bad jokes?

I'M LATE!

You might also be interested in reading questions 11, 13, and 25.

HELLO, FRED!

LATER, TED!

13. Before I was born, where was I? Was I dead?

Maya

Dear Maya,

Your two questions open up fascinating perspectives!

We often wonder about what there will be after life (or after death), but why is it that we don't seem so concerned with what there might have been before? If it is possible that there is an afterlife, could it also be possible that there was once a "beforelife"? Can you imagine an immortality that goes in both directions: forwards and backwards? Could it be that we have always been around, and we will always be around? Wow!

But let's break this down. To answer your first question, we could say that before you were born you were in someone's womb, busy growing. But what about before being in that womb? Before having your body, were you anywhere else? Were you something before existing in a body? And if you didn't have a body, what were you?

We might imagine a kind of paradise prior to our bodily existence where souls would wander, awaiting a body to attach to and be born. We wouldn't be the first to imagine something like this! Do you like the idea?

Your second question, about whether we were dead before birth, almost poses the opposite scenario: a mortality that goes forwards and backwards. Here we might imagine a world where the deceased await their call to live. Living time!

And we can imagine a cycle of death and life, life and death, death and life... and so on, forever. Those storks and those vultures would have a job for eternity!

Of course, we could also reply to both your questions like this— before you were in the womb, you were nothing at all! You didn't exist. And how can we imagine that? You're right, Maya—it's not easy at all!

What if we ask a similar question, but instead of focusing on you, we think about your last birthday cake?
Before it was made, where was the cake?

You might also be interested in reading questions 11 and 12.

14. Is there any way of knowing whether our dead grandparents have feelings?

Mireia

Dear Mireia,

When a grandparent or anyone very close to you dies, you might feel a combination of sadness, outrage, and disbelief. It can seem very hard to believe, understand, and accept that they have disappeared forever. Forever?!

Is it even possible to disappear altogether? Perhaps they are simply somewhere else? But where? And what could they be doing? Are they having fun, eating, thinking, talking? Do they have feelings like they had when they were alive? Can they see us and hear us?

Would we like our dead grandparents to have feelings about everything they see us do and hear us say? What a question! Some people like the idea that our grandparents might be watching us and feel proud of our deeds. Other people find the idea a little unsettling. Would they be watching us ALL the time?

"Not watching us, just keeping us company," say the supporters of the idea of dead grandparents with feelings. "Yes, but if they can feel proud, they could also feel disappointed," object the critics. "What pressure! Not a moment of privacy!"

Maybe it would be better to imagine that they could keep us company, but only when we asked them to. We could invite them to watch a movie, for instance. If we wanted to put their feelings to the test, what movie could we choose? The saddest movie we can think of? The one with the happiest ending? The most upsetting? Or the most hilarious movie of all time?

And what would we say to our dear grandparents, if we could talk to them, while we reach over to grab another handful of popcorn?

You might also be interested in reading questions 10, 18, and 38.

Do you think the grandfather will eat the popcorn?
Or is he just playing?

15. Will we all become extinct one day?

Laura

Dear Laura,

We are not going to beat about the bush: yes. One day, the human species will become extinct. Out of all the animal and plant species that have ever existed on planet Earth, scientists estimate that the vast majority are extinct. And there is frankly no reason to think that most of the species currently living on Earth won't follow the same path.

The appearance and disappearance of species is part of life on Earth, where extinction is the norm and not the exception. But even though all species become extinct, it is true that some species last (much) longer than others. Many species of jellyfish, for example, have been roaming the seas for hundreds of millions of years. Wait a minute! What if we were a spectacularly long-lasting species such as the immortal jellyfish we met in chapter one?

Here we won't beat about the bush either: no. As a mammal species, it would not be realistic to aspire to be quite so long-lived. Paleontological studies suggest that the average duration of mammal species on Earth is a million years, give or take. But not all news is grim. Do you know how long we Homo sapiens have been around? Merely somewhere between 200,000 and 300,000 years. So, we are a fairly young mammal species. If we were to last an average timespan for a mammal, we would still have about 700,000 years left until our extinction. This would mean that neither in our lifetime, Laura, nor in the lifetime of the next few thousand generations of our descendants, would humanity witness its total extinction.

But the longevity of our species could be affected by exceptional, more or less unforeseen circumstances.

Could an asteroid impact, like the one that happened 66 million years ago and caused the extinction of three quarters of all animal and plant species on Earth, including dinosaurs, lead to our extinction? Or the outbreak of a devastating nuclear war? The relentless spread of a deadly pandemic? Or how about the less explosive—but no less inexorable—effects of climate change?

Who knows? Human beings are a very special sort of species. We are more vulnerable than jellyfish, yes. Like all large animals, we require a lot of food, at regular intervals, and this means that any disruption in the food chain would have a fast impact on us. But it is also true that we eat a bit of everything (we are omnivores), which gives us some advantages for survival over species with a more limited diet.

On the other hand, like many other large animals, we reproduce slowly, and produce few offspring at a time, so it would take us quite a while to restore our population in the event of many deaths. But it is also true that we are everywhere and there are many of us. Even in the event of a pandemic or a nuclear war that wiped out 99% of the human population, there would still be 8 million of us left, more than enough to continue the species.

We also have ways of adapting that are not available to other species: we develop technology to fight adverse conditions, we invent tools and form habits to survive better. We can shape the environment to suit our needs. In fact, we are so adaptable that, who knows if we would manage to survive a mass extinction event?

But what if we are just a bit too smart for our own good? So far, the five mass extinctions that have occurred on Earth have had natural causes. What if the next great extinction is already being caused by the Earth-dwelling species known as humans or *Homo sapiens*? Over the last few centuries, many of the changes we have made seeking to put an end to wars, produce more food, make our life easier and improve our wellbeing have generated new threats: nuclear weapons, overpopulation, pandemics, and even climate change.

Until now, we have been able to escape or delay some of these threats with nuclear treaties, vaccines, and the use of renewable energies. But for how long? And what about the impact of our actions on the rest of the species that inhabit planet Earth? Since the arrival of the so-called human civilization, many of the extinctions of species that have occurred and continue to occur at a dizzying rate have been a direct consequence of human activity.

Could it be that we ourselves, with our actions, end up driving our species, and almost all others, to extinction?

And here comes a tough question, Laura. What if the only possibility for the planet to survive was for the human species to disappear? We're not saying this is the case, but what if it were? Can you imagine what Earth would be like if the human species became extinct? Would there be any advantages for the planet if we became extinct? Would there be any disadvantages? In what sense would planet Earth become less valuable if it lost all human beings?

Can you imagine if no species had ever become extinct? What would be the perfect book to read aloud to a saber-toothed tiger?

You might also be interested in reading questions 9 and 32.

16. Why do some people die by suicide?

Laura

Dear Laura,

Suicide is a taboo topic—a difficult issue that is often hidden or covered up, and usually avoided in conversation. But even though it's not comfortable to talk about suicides, it is important for us to. We need to break the taboo.

The first thing to do with a taboo, if we want to break it, is name it, just like you have done in your question by using the word *suicide*. To increase our taboo-breaking power, we can try saying the word out loud: suicide.

The second thing to do if we want to break a taboo is to define the word, so that it is clear what we are talking about: suicide is the act of someone intentionally causing their own death. In short—to die by suicide is to die by taking one's own life.

In this book we have done a third thing to help break the taboo: we have drawn it. The vampire in the illustration is about to die by suicide, having chosen to expose himself to sunlight, after an existence of more than 1,000 years. Why? We could speculate. He may be tired and feel that he has lived "everything" there is to live, and that there's nothing left for him to do. Presented like this, we may even understand the vampire. But real life is not an illustration, and human beings are not vampires.

Everything?
How many years do you think you would have to live to be able to proclaim that you had lived "everything" there is to live? Would it be possible to "live" more in one hundred years than in one thousand? How?

In real life, some people come to feel such unbearable pain in their bodies or in their minds that they become convinced that nothing can be done and that there is no one who can help them. Sometimes, they feel it is impossible to endure the suffering they are experiencing, and this can lead them to believe that the only way of escaping their pain is to take their life and die by suicide.

As you see, when we talk about human beings, unlike when we imagine vampires, our answers and explanations don't seem quite so satisfactory. You might still be asking yourself: yes, yes, but why?

The reasons that lead someone to take their own life are always complex. Each person who dies by suicide does so for different reasons and in different circumstances, so it is not possible to give a single reason as an answer to your question. Some suicides occur after a long road of suffering. In other cases, a suicide may happen more unexpectedly or with no apparent explanation. It is one of the harshest and hardest human phenomena to understand.

When someone close to us dies by suicide, apart from the incomprehension and immense sadness, we might also feel guilt or anger. All these reactions are absolutely normal.

These feelings of incomprehension, sadness, guilt, and anger often come with questions about what happened, some of them very difficult to grapple with. Could I have done something to prevent their suicide? Is it (partly) my fault? Why didn't they seek help? Why did this have to happen to me, to lose my loved one in this way?

Sharing these questions, even in the knowledge that we do not have the answers, is important, because if we keep them to ourselves or hide them, they can be very painful. In any case, one of these questions does have an answer: suicides are never anyone's "fault"; they are not the fault of the person who dies by suicide, nor the fault of their loved ones.

So, what can we do? Talking about suicides and making them visible (breaking the taboo) can help people who have lost someone to suicide to feel less lonely and more supported. On the other hand, it can also help people who have or have had suicidal thoughts to feel that they don't have to keep them secret and encourage them to share their distress.

Some questions stay with us throughout all our lives. They are the kind of questions that help us humans understand ourselves better. Yours, Laura, is one of them. Thank you for opening this door for us to write, and spark questions and conversations about suicide among the readers of this book.

You might also be interested in reading question 31.

If you ever...
... have feelings of despair or suicidal thoughts, or know anyone who does, it is vital to remember that you can talk about it and seek help.

17. Why do we bury the dead?

Àngel

Dear Àngel,

Wondering why we humans do what we do is always fascinating.

Why do you think our ancestors started burying the dead at least 100,000 years ago? What purpose could burying bodies serve?

If you happen to have someone around (a mother, a grandfather, a cousin, or a friend) you could ask them to join you and think about it together. What reasons can you come up with? Why would we bury the dead?

Now keep reading and see if you recognize any of the ideas you came up with (Hello there!) or whether you come across a new idea you hadn't thought of and may even surprise you (Ooooh!).

Burying something is a way of hiding it. By burying a body, we hide it from view and that means that nobody has to witness the decomposition of the body of a loved one. Burying is also a way of hiding something from our sense of smell, to prevent the odor of decomposition from flooding the environment.

Thinking back to the first human burials, it was also a way of hiding the bodies from hungry animals that might otherwise have been attracted to the remains by the scent. This would have been important out of respect for the remains of the deceased person, but also because those very animals may have been dangerous for the rest of the humans in the group (the ones that were still alive and kicking).

Burying a body is also a way of putting it away or removing it from the living areas. Who wants to live with corpses? Among other things, it's a question of space: there's not enough room for us all.

Apart from the question of space, there would have been other reasons for keeping the dead separate from the living. We now know that the bodies of the living are generally much more dangerous than the bodies of the dead (they can give us many more diseases). But throughout history, different people and cultures have thought that decomposing corpses could emit infectious, disease-bearing gases. Burying the bodies was thought to be a way of protecting the living from the perceived dangers of dead bodies.

And of course, it has been a common fear throughout history that the dead might somehow come back, appear before the living (Boooo!), and hurt them in some way. So, bury them! Bury them! Just in case.

The oldest human burials found to date give us more clues. Archaeologists who have carefully studied these burial sites point to the positioning of the bodies, the exact sites chosen for the burials and the objects found next to the skeletons as likely signs that they were buried purposely and carefully. This could be an indication of a belief in some kind of afterlife.

What if I don't like the idea of my body being buried?
There are alternatives. The most common alternative to burial is cremation, also known as incineration, which has in fact overtaken burial as the preferred method of body disposal in many countries. When you cremate a body you place it in a crematorium furnace, where the remains are subjected to a very high temperature and a process of vaporization and high-pressure until they turn to ashes. Once you have the ashes, some people choose to sprinkle them in a place that was special to the deceased person, but do you know what most people do? Yep! They bury them!

Some mythologies and religions have imagined an afterworld in the form of an underworld (like the *Kur*, in Mesopotamian mythology, the *Duat* in Egyptian mythology, or the *Xibalba* of Maya mythology). In this sense, burying the dead underground would also have been a way of easing their transit to the underworld.

The last reason we will mention for burying the dead is perhaps one that we can relate to more easily today. Burying the dead, and marking their burial site, is a way of offering relatives and other loved ones a place to go to grieve, take flowers, stones, or other offerings, and remember their lives. To make it easy to locate the exact place of burial, the tombstones are inscribed with information about the deceased person.

As you can see, Àngel, there are many possible reasons for burying the dead. Did you think of any others?

Woof! Woof!

You might also be interested in reading questions 2, 20, and 21.

18. If someone you love dies, how long are you sad for?

Lorena

Dear Lorena,

Even if we knew exactly when the tears on the page on the left began to fall, it would be impossible to predict when they would stop falling. Will that bath overflow? Splash! Or not?

There is no set duration for the grieving period following the death of a loved one. It depends on so many different factors! It depends on our relationship with the deceased person—were they present in our daily life, or did we only see them very occasionally? It depends on when they died—did they die young, or did they enjoy a long life? And it depends on how they died—was it an expected or an unexpected death? In peaceful or dramatic circumstances?

It also depends on our age when the person dies—we don't express our sadness in the same way when we are 2 years old as when we are 4 or 5, or 12, or 80.

And it also depends on our personality and the opportunities we have to express our pain with words, talk about it, and share our feelings with other empathetic human beings or crocodiles. Each person experiences and expresses their pain for the loss of a loved one in their very own way.

What does tend to happen is that the overwhelming, sweeping sadness we may feel immediately after the death of someone close to us, gradually becomes less intense, less deep, and less constant. This can happen over time and, especially, as we accept the loss of a loved one and learn to live without them. Eventually, the sadness, though it does not necessarily ever disappear completely, ceases to be at the forefront, and we can live our lives fully and enjoyably, even while vividly remembering the loved one we lost.

Is it possible to be sad for "too long"?
If, more than a year after the death of a loved one, someone feels as intensely sad as they felt at the very start, and if their ability to go about their daily life doesn't gradually improve, it may be recommended that they seek counselling.

You might also be interested in reading questions 10, 14, and 38.

19. Is it bad luck to die?

Jóhann

Dear Jóhann,

It is true that sometimes death can seem like a game of chance. Take the case of the Austrian Hans Steininger, more famous for the way he died than for having been the mayor of his town. Hans wore a beard that was as long as some full-grown humans are tall. He carried his beard carefully rolled up in a pocket but would let it loose when he went to bed. One night in 1567, he woke up to find that his building was on fire. He jumped out of bed and ran, desperately fleeing from the flames. But before he could make it out safely, he tripped over his flowing beard, fell down the stairs, and broke his neck. Ouch! Now that is what you call bad luck!

And what do you make of the death of Allan Pinkerton, the founder of the famous detective agency? Having faced and fought off all sorts of bandits and brigands in his lifetime, he died on July 1, 1884, a few days after tripping over the leash of his wife's poodle. When he fell, he bit his tongue so hard and with such bad luck that his teeth, which were in a rather pitiful state, infected the wound and ultimately led to his death. Can you imagine a more absurd death for a top detective?

But a death doesn't have to be quite so absurd to feel like bad luck. When death comes without warning, due to an accident or a natural disaster, for example, it can seem like bad luck. And when someone dies very young, it can also feel like bad luck. Even when someone who is very close to us dies of natural causes at a ripe old age, we might feel it's bad luck.

But dying itself cannot be bad luck, can it? If we all die, does it make sense to say that it's bad luck? Or is it simply a way of saying that death can feel very painful?

You might also be interested in reading questions 6 and 25.

Is it good luck to be born?

20. Why do they dress
the dead in white
in India and Pakistan?

Afiya

Dear Afiya,

Can you believe that alongside your question we found this other
one sent to us by Hugo: "Why is the color black associated with
death?" Two questions made for each other! It's funny that for some
people the color of death and mourning is white, while for others
it's black.

When someone dies, family and friends perform rituals and hold
celebrations where they get together and say good-bye to the
deceased person. The body of the deceased person is washed and
dressed; gatherings or wakes are held at people's houses or funeral
homes; offerings are brought to the grave; and all kinds of religious
and non-religious ceremonies are held. These are part of the funeral
rites that exist in all human communities to help us express and
share our grief (the pain of losing a loved one).

Every place in the world, every culture, every religion (and even
every family) has its own rites and rituals, and one of the most
interesting differences is precisely what you and Hugo point
out—color!

As you rightly say, Afiya, white is used in India and Pakistan, but
also in many other places across Asia. In the case of India, where
the majority religion is Hinduism, they don't only dress the dead in
white. Traditionally, people attending a funeral also wear this color.
White is associated with the pallor of death and symbolizes purity,
light, and hope for a death that is thought of as the beginning
of another life. In Pakistan, which is a predominantly Muslim
country, corpses are wrapped in a white sheet or shroud. However,
people attending the funeral can wear other colors, preferably sober
ones. They also refrain from wearing jewelry and accessories and
try to dress as simply as possible.

In Europe, on the other hand, and in many other countries, as Hugo points out, the color associated with mourning and death is black. At burials and funerals, people tend to wear black or dark colors as a way of showing respect to the deceased person and their loved ones. In some countries, such as Spain and Italy, until relatively recently (and in some cases still today), it was traditional for widows and widowers to dress in mourning clothes. For a period after the death of their spouse, they wore black as a sign of mourning. And why black? Black, which is the absence of light, is related to darkness, the unknown, pain and the mystery of death.

But even though the use of the color black to mark mourning dates back to ancient Rome, the colors associated with mourning and death have changed over the centuries, and not always for religious reasons. Economy and fashion have also played an interesting role. In medieval Europe, for instance, the color of mourning was primarily white. Apart from the symbolism of the color, the truth is that white fabric was the cheapest (it didn't need to be dyed) and people usually had something white to wear in their wardrobe. At a certain point, wealthier people started attending funerals dressed first in purple, and then in black, to show that they could afford fabric treated with expensive dyes. And that's the way fashion trends begin!

And are they no other colors associated with death? Oh yes! At an Ashanti funeral in Ghana, the relatives of the deceased person usually wear red and black, symbolizing death and sorrow. Other guests may wear black or white, or both colors at the same time. White is typically worn on the occasion of the death of an elderly person, in celebration of a long and admirable life.

But when it comes to colors and death, Mexico takes the crown! The altars prepared by the living to honor their dead on *Día de los Muertos* (Day of the Dead) are bursting with vibrant colors. Orange, purple, and black stand out, but you'll also find white, pink, blue, green, and red. Why so many colors? Each color has its own symbolic meaning. For example, orange is the color of mourning in Aztec mythology, and it's believed to be the only color the deceased can see on their journey back to the world of the living; purple represents Catholic mourning; and pink symbolizes the joy of the living to be reunited with the deceased. Beyond the symbolism of the different colors, if we compare this festive explosion of color with the sobriety and solemnity of black and white, could it tell us something interesting about different attitudes to death and to the dead?

What other colors do you think we could use to dress the dead?

You might also be interested in reading questions 17 and 22.

21. Does death have a physical appearance?

Amanda

Dear Amanda,

If you are wondering whether death might jump out from behind a corner and say hello, you need not worry. Death doesn't have a physical appearance in that way. Death is a process or a state, and it doesn't have a shape.

But it's curious that throughout history, human beings have insisted on giving death a physical appearance, and often the way we imagine it is in the form of a humanlike figure. Could it be that we need to personify death, to see if that might help us understand it better?

As soon as we read your question, an army of skeletons, skulls, grim reapers, angels, and dark robed figures came to mind. We recalled tales, legends, paintings, books, movies, and videogames where death appears in various physical forms.

Representations of death are found on vases, papyruses, mosaics, manuscripts, tombstones and buildings of many ancient civilizations and peoples. If we look at the way death has been depicted in art, popular culture and folklore throughout history, we will find many different shapes and forms, dressed in all sorts of clothing.

In ancient Rome, fate (and therefore death) was represented by the Fates: three young sisters in charge of spinning and cutting the threads of human lives. With Christianity, they evolved into the figure of the Grim Reaper, which, from the 15th century, started to be represented as a skeleton shrouded in a black cloak, with a scythe always at the ready.

Representations of death are generally dismal. They appear in darkness or in moments of chaos (like battles or epidemics) and their appearance is almost always terrifying or at the very least fearsome. Apart from the representation of the Grim Reaper, death can come in the form of a skeleton with a rotating head riding a carriage pulled by pale horses, ready to collect corpses, like the *Ankou* of the ancient Celts. Or it might appear as the *Giltiné* of ancient Baltic legends, in the form of an ugly old woman, with a long nose and a deadly poisonous tongue. And what about the *Dullahan* from Irish folklore? A headless horseman, often carrying his head under his arm. Shudder!

But there are also other, friendlier representations, like Father Time, depicted as an old, bearded man, often with wings, who carries some kind of clock as well as a scythe. He sometimes accompanies the Grim Reaper, but is far less threatening, almost huggable, as if he simply wanted to whisper a gentle reminder that time (and life) goes by.

If you had to cast the character of death in a play, which of the four representations from the previous page would you choose? Or would you prefer to imagine a new physical appearance for death, complete with its own wardrobe and all? What would your death character look like?

One of the least terrifying and most gentle representations of death...
... that we know of appears in the book Duck, Death and the Tulip, by Wolf Erlbruch. Try to find a copy at your library or bookshop, read it, and see what you think!

You might also be interested in reading question 28.

22. How do they make tombstones?

Sira

Dear Sira,

At last! An easy question to answer! Thank you!

As the name gives away, tombstones are normally made of... stone.

Ever since we started burying our dead, humans have sought different ways of covering the tombs. What for? To make sure that the dead didn't wake up and wander out for a nighttime walk (ha!) or, more seriously, to seal the tomb and prevent scavengers from accessing the remains. Throughout history, different materials have been used to cover tombs, such as quicklime, branches, logs, or stones and small rocks. There you have the origin and one of the functions of tombstones: to seal the tomb.

But tombstones like the one you see in the illustration (which doesn't cover the tomb, but rather stands vertically at the head of the tomb) are usually called headstones and have a different function: to signpost the place where the person is buried and make it easy for their relatives to find their burial site in the cemetery. They also provide a place for relatives to mourn and commemorate the life of their loved one or ancestor.

So how do they make them? First of all, the stone is carved to size. Then it is sculpted, decorated, and engraved with the name and dates of birth and death of the person who is buried there. Engraving is one of the trickier parts of the process. In the past, stonemasons would engrave the letters by hand. They'd chisel them out, then pour molten iron over the grooves so that it would be readable. Today, most of the lettering is engraved mechanically. They also often engrave a photograph of the deceased person (this can now be laser engraved from a computer file) or they may even engrave a drawing of the face of the deceased person or any other drawing in memory of them. Once the slab is ready, it is taken to the cemetery, where it is placed in the ground, or over a niche, as a cover, depending on the type of burial.

And who makes all these tombstones? Well, that's a whole other story.

You might also be interested in reading questions 17, 20, and 38.

23. Why aren't children allowed to see the dead?

Fernanda

Dear Fernanda,

Has it ever happened to you that you wanted to see a deceased loved one, but you were not allowed to? How did you feel? Did you ask why? And were you given an explanation?

Seeing a dead body is a very clear way of understanding what happens when someone dies and their body stops working. But it can also be an impactful experience. Some adults think that seeing a dead body might be too distressing for children. They believe that not allowing younger kids to see the dead is a way of protecting them.

It is true that even some adults would rather not see the lifeless bodies of their loved ones. They would prefer to keep in their memories moments when the person was still alive, so they can think of them as they were in those shared moments, rather than through the memory of a body without energy, movement, or voice.

However, many people feel that seeing the deceased person helps them understand their death better.

After reading this, do you think you would prefer to see the body of a loved one or not? Does it depend? What does it depend on?

In any case it is interesting to think that if you had been born at a different time or in a different place, you might have already seen more than one dead body. In the past (and still today in some places), the dead were laid out in homes, where adults and children would say goodbye to their loved ones in the very same places they had lived together. What do you think about that?

In contrast with your experience, take what is known as *famadihana* ... or "turning of the bones," a funerary ceremony of the Magalasy people in Madagascar whereby, every seven years, they exhume the bodies of their ancestors, rewrap them in new shrouds, and lift them in a dance to live music, before re-burying them for another seven years. Children take part in the ceremony, in an opportunity to learn all about their ancestors.

You might also be interested in reading questions 24 and 28.

24. Why do people find it uncomfortable to talk about death?

Michael

Dear Michael,

Thank you for such a delightfully uncomfortable question!

You are right—it's not easy to find people who aren't uncomfortable when it comes to talking about death. Do you know anyone?

The fact is that talking about death is not easy. It can cause pain, anxiety, fear, or sadness. And who wants to cause all that? Nobody, of course! How uncomfortable! But it's funny, because precisely being able to talk about death can help us cope with the pain, the anxiety, the fear, and the sadness.

The chance to talk about death calmly can help us understand it better, share our concerns, and express our curiosity. Imagine being able to think of death as if it was just another part of life, and being able to talk naturally about what it feels like when we lose someone we love deeply, about how we would like our funeral to be, about what we would like to remember about someone when they die, or what we would like others to remember about us when we die.

But, as your question suggests, death is a difficult topic. Why is that? Might it be because talking about death reminds us that one day we will die, and we find that scary? Is it because it reminds us that people who we love will disappear one day, and we find that painful? Could it be that ignoring death and pretending it doesn't exist makes us feel a little less anxious? As if never talking about death might make it disappear? (Death? What's that?), or as if talking about death could actually make it appear (Eeek!).

With this book, we are trying to encourage more people to talk about death naturally. Do you think we will succeed?

You might also be interested in reading questions 23 and 28.

FRIENDLY REMINDER
Talking about death does not cause death.

25. Is there any fate worse than death?

Ali

Dear Ali,

It is interesting to think about the difference between your question and this other question: "Is there anything worse than death?" It might be easier to answer the second question than it is to answer yours. Greek mythology offers us fabulous examples of existences that we might consider to be far worse than death.

Prometheus, punished by the Greek god Zeus for stealing fire from the gods and giving it to humans, spends eternity chained to a rock. A whole eternity of suffering! For Tantalus, another misbehaving Greek god, Zeus also devised an eternity of a very special kind— he sent him to live in a pool surrounded by trees brimming with fruits that disappear every time he reaches for one, and water that recedes every time he tries to drink it. Eternal hunger and thirst!

We are sure that more than one person reading this book would seriously consider choosing death over these existences of perpetual suffering!

But your question specifically mentions "fate." And that makes us think of the experience of living while knowing that death is our ultimate fate, and that, with absolute certainty, one day we will die.

It is not easy to image what our life would be like if we had a fate other than death. Can you imagine our lives if they were eternal, for example? Would it be a better fate or a worse fate? Can you imagine any other fate that was neither death nor eternal life?

You might also be interested in reading questions 12 and 19.

They say that...
... stepping on poop with your left foot brings good luck, but not enough to spare us from death. (Also, is the man about to step on the poop with his left foot or with his right foot?)

26. If I die, who will get to keep my game console?

Gael

Dear Gael,

What a practical question! And even though you might not think so (because of the console), what an ancient question! Ankh-Ren asked himself almost the very same question about 4,000 years ago in ancient Egypt. His is the first written will we have a record of, and we know he left all his belongings to his brother Uah. Shortly after, Uah drew up his own will, in which he left his wife everything his brother Ankh-Ren had left him in the first will.

And from one will to another, we come to you, Gael, and your console. Like you, Ankh-Ren must have wondered: when I die, what will become of all my things? Who will get to keep them? Will anyone appreciate them as much as I do? Are there any rules or traditions when it comes to leaving your belongings to other people? Wait! Is it up to me to decide whom I would like to leave my belongings to?

It's time to think about drafting a will. But it will not do to simply write it down on any old piece of paper. A Last Will and Testament is a legal document that specifies in detail whom we want to leave our things to when we die. The people we leave our belongings to are called *heirs* and the belongings passed on (for example, your console) are what you call the *inheritance*.

Think about it, Gael, because whatever becomes of your console is in fact in your hands! But how will you decide whom to leave it to? Who would deserve it more? Who would enjoy it more? Who would take better care of it? And whose life would it change the most?

Heirs are usually relatives or very close friends. But not necessarily. In 2007, a Portuguese aristocrat, Mr. Noronha Cabral da Câmara, bequeathed his immense fortune to seventy people randomly chosen from the telephone directory. A notary public validated the process, and that is how the very surprised heirs were able to receive their share of the unexpected inheritance. Mr. Noronha seems to have got the inspiration from an old film by Ernst Lubitsch called *If I Had a Million*, where something similar happens.

Whatever we might decide, leaving a written will makes things much easier after our death, because our will is clearly stated in writing and it's easier to distribute our belongings and money. But sometimes there is no written will. It may be because the person did not expect to die soon, because they preferred not to decide how to distribute their assets, or simply because time passed, and death came before they could get around to drafting a will. In these cases, it is the law that regulates how the belongings of the deceased person should be distributed. And then, yes, the law does establish that the inheritance goes to the closest relatives.

Sometimes there may be no family or no specific person or people to leave an inheritance to. In those cases, some people choose to leave their belongings to their town or city, or to a charitable cause. If there is neither a will nor any close relatives to claim the inheritance, the person's assets all go to the state.

Sometimes inheritances can get complicated. For example, when it is unclear whether a person has died or not. When someone disappears and their body is not found, a certain number of years must go by before a judge can certify that the person is dead. Only when such a certification is issued can the will be executed, and the inheritance be distributed.

In the wills of Ankh-Ren and Uah…
… there is no mention of any console (can you imagine?), but there is a specific detail that stands out. In both wills, three categories of assets are listed: properties (houses), other belongings, and slaves. Times change, fortunately, and today, in addition to being able to play with consoles, nobody can own another person as property.

It may seem that receiving something in inheritance is always a good thing. Many inheritances have made heirs millionaires! But did you know that it is also possible to inherit debt? Can you imagine having to pay for things you didn't buy and don't even want? Or simply for debts incurred that have absolutely nothing to do with you?

It can also happen that you inherit assets, but the costs of accepting the inheritance are greater than the value of the assets. In these cases, you can renounce the inheritance. But as you can see, inheriting is not always as easy as we might think.

Of course, when it's a console or objects that don't have huge value, it's easier. A legal will is not normally required in these cases. Family and friends can distribute small items of sentimental value and yes, in this case, even a handwritten note on an old piece of paper might do.

You might also be interested in reading question 34.

27. How can you tell if you will die soon?

Eloi

Dear Eloi,

Knock! Knock! Knock! Three knocks on the door. "Who's there?" you ask. Nobody answers, so you open the door and peek out. You look one way and the other. There is no one there. Now imagine that this scene is part of a horror movie. Nothing good is about to happen, that much we know! Could it be, as superstition has it, a sign that death is around the corner?

Omens of death, alleged signs that announce a death, date back to ancient times and are still today very much present in the popular folklore of many cultures around the world. And in horror movies too, of course!

A hen crowing like a rooster? A black cat meowing at midnight? An owl hooting while we are lying in bed? A clock stopping or suddenly restarting again after years? A mirror falling from the wall? Bells tolling on their own at night? Omens of death are unsurprisingly always unsettling and often terrifying.

The extent to which you can tell that death is near...
...might also depend on the person in question. Some people are perceptive and observant, while others won't even look up from their book.

Some of these omens were quite specific as to the time it would take for death to arrive (two days, a week, or before the Earth goes round the Sun again), but in most cases they were not (something was going to happen "soon" and that was it). Oh, Eloi! It's hard to decide which is worse. Precision or ambiguity? What would you prefer?

So, going back to your question: Can you tell that you will die soon or that death is near? If we try to answer this question based on current medical knowledge, we will find that there is more than one answer. Each death is a different case, and what each person may feel before they die is also different.

Some deaths occur suddenly and are difficult to notice in any way before they happen. But other deaths, especially those following an illness, may come in a less sudden manner. Doctors specializing in what is known as palliative care (the care and attention provided to patients with serious uncurable illnesses at the end of their lives) say that, in those cases, it is possible to know the proximity of death fairly clearly a few days or even weeks before it happens. And how is it exactly that they can tell? What are some of the signs? Patients may feel their body weaken to the extent that they can no longer do things they could do before, like walking, and they may even need help to change their position in bed or to drink water. They begin to spend more and more time asleep. There may be some confusion and sometimes, patients may experience hallucinations. Towards the very end, they are barely able to eat, drink, or swallow medications, blood pressure drops, breathing changes, and they spend most of the time asleep. These are some of the signs that indicate that death is very near.

Of course, not everyone will experience all those symptoms or changes. The specific symptoms will depend on each illness and the person's overall health condition. And it is very important to clarify that these symptoms are not necessarily a sign of imminent death (they can appear for other reasons that have nothing to do with death).

Some of the things we notice when we are dying may cause more discomfort than others. For the most uncomfortable symptoms (if any), such as nausea, pain, or more labored breathing, there are medications and treatments that can help.

You might also be interested in reading questions 6, 28, and 29.

28. Is death scary?

Christian

Dear Christian,

Some people are so afraid of death that they are even scared to talk about it. They hear the word "death", and they pretend they haven't heard it, change the subject or run to hide until the "danger" is over.

Death, as a topic of conversation, as an idea we have to live with, and as a future outlook, sends shivers down many people's spines.

The truth is that death gives us many reasons to feel slightly scared. To start with, nobody knows what happens after death. It is the greatest uncertainty of all our uncertainties. And uncertainty itself can be frightening. Humans like to understand things, and death is something we will never be able to fully understand. At least not while we are alive!

The fact that we won't know how or when we will die is another type of uncertainty that can also be scary and give us a sense of lack of control. It's hard to live with something quite so unpredictable!

The idea of ceasing to exist is also scary. Even if we believe in an afterlife, there is always room for doubt. The idea of vanishing altogether can be rather unsettling. If we believe in an afterlife with some kind of paradise and some kind of hell, we may also fear not having behaved well enough during our life on Earth. And even if we don't believe in an afterlife, there is always room for doubt too.

Another reason why we may fear death has more to do with the people whom we leave behind than with our own death. Will they manage without us?

On the other hand, we may be scared that our loved ones might die. We are afraid to imagine a life without them. What will I do when they are gone? How can I make sure I never forget their voices? What will life without them be like? Will it be very painful?

But perhaps what is most frightening is the process of dying itself and what might happen to us while we are dying. How will I die? Will it hurt? Will it be a long process? Will I suffer? Will I be with people I love? Will I realize that I am dying? And what will it feel like, to know that I am dying?

Interestingly, for some people, the fear of (their own) death gradually decreases as they get older. It may strike us as odd, because we might think that the older we are and the closer we are to death, the scarier it might seem. But apparently, as death approaches, some people become more accepting of death as the end of life, and of the fact that theirs is not far away.

For others, the fear does not decrease quite so much, but most people manage to live with it.

Fear of death is only concerning if it is so intense and irrational that it prevents us from leading a normal life. For example, if we start to avoid leaving the house in case a flowerpot falls on our head and kills us, then, it's probably time to seek help!

But asking ourselves questions about death and occasionally feeling a bit scared is perfectly normal if you are a human being.

What we should not be afraid of is talking about death. On the contrary! It is the only way we have of sharing and processing what really scares us about it.

And what about poor old death? What could it possibly be afraid of?

You might also be interested in reading questions 21, 23, 24, and 27.

29. What does it feel like to be poisoned?

Fernando

Dear Fernando,

Fortunately, we do not speak from experience! We had to do some research. And the answer to your question, like to many others, is that it depends. What you feel when you are poisoned depends on the poison in question, on how much poison we are dealing with, and on how the poison is administered.

The most important factor? Quantity. Some substances are so dangerous that just a few drops or even less can cause death, while others are only dangerous in much larger amounts. That is why when people talk about poisons, they talk about the *lethal dose*: the minimum amount necessary for a specific substance to be deadly.

The method of administration is also an important factor. Some poisons are lethal with just a lick, while others need to be injected for them to have any effect.

Each poison causes a specific set of symptoms. Some poisons cause terrible pain, spasms, dizziness, cramps, and violent convulsions. Others trigger a sudden collapse of the body, causing heart attacks or comas. There are even some poisons that, when administered very gradually, act almost imperceptibly. The perfect crime!

But did you know, Fernando, that by far most poisonings are accidental and happen in the home? Yes, our enemies are right in our homes! And we are not talking about cobras or tarantulas, brown recluse spiders or Asian hornets. The main culprits are plain old cleaning products (like bleach) and medications, those where you can read the warning "keep out of reach of children."

You might also be interested in reading questions 6, 27, and 36.

Did you know that...
... some poisons that would be fatal in large amounts can be beneficial or even serve as medication to relieve or cure diseases when administered in small doses?

30. When I go to sleep, how do I know that I haven't died?

Zian

Dear Zian,

In dreams, knowledge and imagination intertwine in such a way that makes them difficult to untangle. It's not easy to work out what we know or don't know when we are asleep!

The only test we can come up with to answer your question would be to wait and see if you wake up. If you wake up, you can be certain that you were only sleeping and not dead. Or can you?

Another of the questions we received for this book was: "Are we sure that at night we don't die and then come back to life in the morning?" The test gets more and more complicated!

Perhaps you could ask someone for a favor. Next time you go to sleep, you could ask them to check and see if you are dead or just sleeping. How could they do that? They could approach you and get close enough to check if they can sense your breathing (the sound and the slight movement of your chest, nose, or mouth). If there was no sign of breathing, they could take your hand and check for your pulse on your wrist or put their ear to your chest to listen for your heartbeat. If there was no sign of a heartbeat, and as a very last resource, they may just have to resort to pinching.

A good pinch would wake up anyone who was asleep! And, as far as we know, no pinch has ever brought anyone back from the dead.

Pay close attention to the illustration...
... is it possible that the vampire's teddy bear has just been revived thanks to a pinch by his owner?

Even though sleeping and dying are very different things, they are similar enough for humans to have linked them together in our imagination for millennia.

It's no coincidence that the Greek gods of sleep (Hypnos) and death (Thanatos) were twin brothers. Nor is it surprising that in many religions death is referred to as an "eternal sleep" or "eternal rest." Or that when someone dies, we say "rest in peace." Did you know that the word cemetery comes from the ancient Greek word *koimeterion*, meaning "place for sleeping?"

It is hardly surprising either that we have invented all those fairy tales where characters sleep for years and then wake up, like Sleeping Beauty or Snow White. Or all those stories about the living dead, vampires, and zombies. The connection between sleep and death intrigues us, unsettles us, and sparks interesting questions like yours.

But what are those similarities that make us join them together in our imagination?

One of the most obvious similarities between sleep and death is immobility. When we die, our body remains still and does not react to stimuli. When we sleep, our body enters a state of rest and can remain still for reasonably long periods of time. There are even some phases of deep sleep where we barely react to external stimuli, and it can be harder to wake us up (the pinch required to wake us up would have to be extra strong). But even though from the outside it might seem that we are not moving, we are actually moving. And most importantly: our organism remains active even though it is at rest. When we are dead, this is not the case.

Another similarity may have something to do with darkness. We tend to imagine death as a fade to black. When we close our eyes to fall asleep, it might seem that the same thing happens. The world disappears! Or we disappear!

Imagine what it's like for babies, who think, for the first few months of their life, that the only things that exist are what they see; and that what they stop seeing ceases to exist. How terrifying it must be when they close their eyes to go to sleep! "Is the world over? Am I over?" Baby bursts into tears (waaah!, waaah!), but baby immediately hears the sound of the lullaby being sung to her and lets that voice arriving from the world she can no longer see take her to sleep, until she opens her eyes again tomorrow and sees the world is still there.

Thank goodness! After all, sleep is a temporary state of rest. It doesn't last forever, we can wake up, and in fact, we do tend to wake up quite easily, without anyone having to pinch us. Death, however, is permanent, and there's no waking up from that. Unless you turn into a zombie, of course!

You might also be interested in reading question 5.

31. What's the meaning of life if we are going to die?

Luz Mary

WHAT'S THE MEANING OF LIFE IF I'M NEVER GOING TO DIE?

Dear Luz Mary,

Your question seems to imply that if we never died (if we lived forever), life would be more meaningful. Out of curiosity, we would like to ask you what meaning you think eternity would bring to life? And why do you think death takes away meaning from life?

Have you noticed that our dear vampire raises the exact opposite question? His question seems to imply that if he were going to die one day, his life would be more meaningful. And also out of curiosity, we would like to ask him what meaning he thinks death would bring to his life. And why does he think eternity takes away meaning from life?

Although these two questions seem to be opposite to each other, in fact they inquire into the same mystery. What is this strange life? What are we doing here? Why are we here, and what are we here for?

On the one hand, if we know we are going to die and nothing lasts, we might wonder whether, in the grand scheme of things, anything we do in our life actually matters. What difference does what we do make? But on the other hand, knowing that our life is short and will end, we could take it as a sort of challenge: will we be capable of giving meaning to our life in the short time we have on Earth?

It may be easier to think of points that are small and modest but pleasant and meaningful than to think of A SINGLE GREAT AND COMPLETE POINT TO IT ALL. Let's try: what ten things would you like to do before you die?

Some questions about the meaning of life to wonder and ponder over: Are some lives more meaningful than others? Is your life more meaningful than the life of a fly? And the life of a cypress tree? Does the life of an important scientist have more meaning than yours or the same meaning? What things bring meaning to our lives? Are they always the same things or do they change over time? Does everyone find the meaning of life in the same things? Is it necessary to find a meaning to life? Or can one live well without ever entirely working out the meaning of life?

You might also be interested in reading question 16.

32. In the future, will there be special machines that bring the dead back to life?

Núria

Dear Núria,

Imagine a 14th century Núria wondering the same thing: "In the future, will there be special machines that bring the dead back to life?" Now imagine that this Núria from the past is presented with the extraordinary opportunity to travel to the future in a time machine. All the way to the 21st century! By sheer coincidence, in the exact place where her 14th-century house once stood, there is now a large hospital. Núria lands precisely in one of the operating rooms, just in time to witness how a surgeon administers a controlled electric discharge with a defibrillator to a patient in cardiac arrest and apparently dead. Then, they manage to "bring him back from the dead." "What is that magical machine!"

What we mean to say is: what if this is already the future?! What if there already are machines that could bring people back from the dead?

113

For the Núria from the past and also for the doctors of her time, when the heart stopped it meant death had occurred. If the heart had stopped beating, there was nothing to be done. But a few centuries later, in the 18th century, it came to be observed that in cases of drowning, for example, it could happen that people who were apparently dead (whose heart had stopped) were not in fact permanently dead. In other words, it was possible to "bring them back from the dead" or revive them. Are you ready to read about some of the methods for bringing people back from the dead that were put to the test? There was rubbing, slapping (!), massaging, changing the position of the body, throwing freezing water on them, or hanging the person upside down to release the water from their lungs. Some of the techniques they tried out are hard to believe, like the one whereby they tied the person across the back of a horse and made it trot so that the movement would give them a cardiac massage and facilitate air entering and exiting the lungs.

By the mid-19th century, to the great fortune of people apparently dead who were "brought back," there was more focus on techniques such as cardiac massage, opening the airway, and assisted ventilation (all of them techniques that are part of what is now known as *cardiopulmonary resuscitation* or *CPR maneuvers*).

And what about machines? There have been many, such as the Biomotor invented by Rudolf Eisenmenger in 1903—an artificial respiration device indicated for the resuscitation of patients in cardiorespiratory arrest caused by drowning or intoxication. Or the device that delivered small electric discharges to the heart to try to restore normal heart rate (the defibrillator) that Claude Beck used for the first time successfully in 1947 on a 14-year-old patient who had suffered a cardiac arrest at the end of a surgical procedure.

But the defibrillator Beck used doesn't bear much resemblance to the one time-travelling Núria sees in our story. Defibrillators have come a long way in the last century or so. For one, they are also much smaller and portable compared to the first heavy old hulks. This means not only that ambulances can be fitted with them, but that many public spaces are also equipped with portable defibrillators, which are easy to use without the need for a doctor.

All that knowledge and the use of new techniques and devices changed the concept of death forever. When the heart stopped, it no longer necessarily meant death!

Today, what defines death is the cessation of brain activity, which is a quick and (apparently) irreversible process. But might that change in the future? Could we someday find ways of slowing down or reversing the process? Will science redefine death again in the future? We will have to wait some time (or perhaps travel in time) before we can answer that question!

SAY CHEESE, DANTE!

Can you imagine...
... being able to revive a woman from the Stone Age to see how she might adapt to the modern world? Or how about your great grandfather, so you can ask him how your grandmother behaved when she was little? How about great authors from the past for them to sign their books? How much do you think a fresh signature of a 14th century writer would be worth? If it were possible, who would you like to bring back from the dead?

You might also be interested in reading questions 3, 5, and 15.

33. Why don't they give people an injection to help them die when they are sick, like they do with animals?

Marc

Dear Marc,

When a pet is suffering from a painful, incurable illness or disease, you are right that it is common to put an end to their life with a quick and painless method to prevent further suffering.
In other words, animal euthanasia is performed. *Euthanasia* is a word that comes from ancient Greek and means "good death."

Good death?! Can death ever be good? The idea behind this common practice with animals is that some deaths are indeed, if not "good," certainly better than others. And that, sometimes, when an animal is destined to suffer a painful and agonizing death (a bad death), intervening medically to procure them a good (or better) death is an act of compassion. Killing out of compassion? Something along those lines, yes.

In fact, if we give your question a gentle scratch, Marc, we might find another underlying question that is closely related to this—why wouldn't we show the same "compassion" for human beings?

But there is an important difference. Whereas animal euthanasia, though not without critics, is broadly accepted, in the case of human euthanasia, society's opinion is much more divided. It raises more doubts. Indeed, as you suggest in your question, in most countries, *active euthanasia* (administering a drug intravenously or by any other means to end a human's life) is prohibited by law. In other countries, *passive euthanasia* (suspending a medical treatment that was keeping a gravely or incurably ill patient alive) is also prohibited. However, there are some countries—which are in fact growing in number—where both kinds of euthanasia are legally permitted. In those countries, patients suffering from severe, incurable, or terminal illnesses can ask their medical team to help them die if they wish to do so.

Like all matters of life and death, euthanasia elicits strong feelings and conflicting ideas. It also gives rise to hard questions. Can you think of any particularly difficult questions about euthanasia?

You might also be interested in reading questions 8 and 25.

34. Why do some people donate their organs when they die?

Nataly

Dear Nataly,

Usually, when we talk about donating or giving, objects or cash come to mind.

But one of our body organs?!—it sounds like something out of science fiction! Is it really that easy to remove an organ from one body and put it into another?

Perhaps "easy" is not the word. In fact, when an organ is placed into a body it doesn't belong to, the body may recognize the new organ as an invader and go into full attack mode: "Get rid of the foreign organ!!" That is why not just any person's organ will do: they must be compatible. And that is also why we had to wait until drugs were developed to prevent bodies from rejecting foreign organs before seeing the first successful transplant of an internal organ. It happened in 1954, in Boston, and involved a kidney transplant from one identical twin brother to another (how's that for compatibility!). However, unlike the people in your question, both twins were alive.

To be able to transplant organs from a dead body to a living body, the world had to wait for the invention of the artificial respirator. It made it possible to keep alive the organs of a person with brain death by maintaining oxygen supply. So, when someone with healthy organs dies, if doctors act quickly, they can remove the organs that are still alive from their body and place them in bodies of people who need organs that function better than their own, thereby saving and prolonging their lives, or improving their quality of life.

When a healthy person dies, they can donate (hold on tight!): two kidneys, one liver, one heart, two lungs, one pancreas, and their intestines—a total of eight vital organs. A single donor can save the lives of up to eight different people.

Donating organs is a way of gifting life and that is why many people choose to do so. Isn't it beautiful to think that parts of you, even though you are dead and will not be there to witness it, can help other people to go on living?

Some questions
If I donate an organ to someone else, does that person become a little bit "me"? Or not really? If it is possible to donate my organs to save lives when I die, is it my duty to do so, or is it not quite a duty? Why?

You might also be interested in reading question 26.

35. Is there anywhere where you can look up when you are going to die?

Lucas

Dear Lucas,

As soon as we read your intriguing question, a thousand more questions popped into our heads: What would this place full of death dates be like? Do you imagine it as a cave up on a remote mountain? Or would it be more like a huge office building in the middle of a big city? Would there be a single place where the death dates of every living being on the planet were kept? Or would each country or region have its own cave or office? Who would write down the dates? Where would they get the information from? And how would they know that it was reliable? Do you think it would be in the interest of human beings to know when we were going to die? If such a place existed, would you go? And would you believe the death date they gave you?

As you may well know, you are not the first human to imagine such a place. The idea is related to the belief that the future is already written and that everything is already set out from the moment we are born. It's called destiny! The idea dates back to antiquity and can be found in many religious and spiritual beliefs from all over the world. Take the Greek and Egyptian oracles, for example. The oracles were individuals (priests and prophets) with the alleged gift of seeing the future thanks to inspiration from the gods. People used to go and consult the oracle with all sorts of questions: "Will I be happy in this marriage?" "Will I have any children?" "Will my business be successful?" or (you guessed it, Lucas!) "When will I die?"

But the oracles didn't give dates or details that were too specific. They gave their answers in the form of prophecies that resembled impossible riddles, rather than information. As if knowledge about the future was dangerous to share too clearly, or as if they wanted to avoid getting caught not knowing!

Even today, many humans still find the idea of being able to know the future irresistibly attractive. In the 21st century people still sell (and buy) divination services such as palmistry (reading the palm of the hand as a way of foretelling the future) or cartomancy (card reading).

However, we regret to inform you that if we rely on current science and technology, no crystal ball or other contraption has yet been invented that allows us to know the future, let alone specific details about the future. So, the answer to your question is: no. There is nowhere where you can look up when you are going to die.

It is true that sometimes doctors, in the case of certain illnesses, can tell if death is near, and then they can give an (approximate) idea of when a patient might die. But, there's no way of predicting death if a person is healthy.

However, that does not mean we know nothing at all! For example, we know that there are many factors that influence the number of years a person can be expected to live. We know than women, on average, live longer than men (about 5 or 6 years longer). We also know that a baby born today in a rich country, with political and social stability, like Monaco, has a much higher chance of living a long life (an average of 87 years) than a baby born today in an unstable country, with high levels of poverty and population displaced by constant natural disasters and drought, like Chad (an average of 55 years).

Back in the Viking times in Norway...
... there were some priests who were said to have the power to speak with the goddess of death, Hela, who knew the destinies of every warrior. But these priests were forbidden to reveal any details about those deaths. Shhh!

We know that, even within the same country, babies born into affluent families will live (on average) longer than babies born into families with scarce resources. And we also know that, even within the same level of wealth within a given country, differences in diet and exercise can impact the length of a life.

Taking into account all these factors and data on all births and deaths in the world, every year the World Health Organization publishes their life expectancy indices for all countries in the world (you can look it up!). This is probably the closest we can get to having somewhere where we can look up "when we are going to die." But guess what! Life expectancy increases as we grow older. For instance, a man born in the US in 1957, had a life expectancy of 66.5 years when he was born. With every birthday, his life expectancy has readjusted. By his 65th birthday, his life expectancy had risen to 77.9 years (an extra 14.5 years!), and if he happens to live beyond that, to the age of 80, his life expectancy will readjust again, to about 87 or 88 years.

The date of our death cannot be written from birth for us to look up, because, besides the possibility of having an accident or suffering illnesses, the way we live and what we experience affects the length of our life.

Just imagine the poor person in charge at the cave or the office, having to correct millions and millions of death dates every year!

You might also be interested in reading questions 7 and 8.

36. Is it true that if you are decapitated, your body can run around headless?

Mishal

Dear Mishal,

They say so many things about death! They say that when we die our hair and nails keep growing. They say a chopped off head can speak or look surprised, and they say that the body the surprised head belonged to might finish a race after being severed halfway to the finish line, like your question seems to suggest. And here we have a question for you: if the headless body won the race, would the head change its surprised expression for an expression of joy at the victory?

Popular culture is full of myths about death. Often, they are stories with a touch of dark humor, perfect for telling at nighttime around a campfire. Other stories come from misunderstandings or mistaken ideas. For example, it is not that the hair, the beard, or the nails grow, but rather than when we die, our skin dries out and, as it does, it recedes and exposes some of the hair and the nails that were previously beneath the skin. They seem to grow, but not really.

And what about chopped-off heads, then? Do you know the incredible story of Mike, who, around the mid-20th century, lived eighteen months without a head? Not only did he run about, but he also ate, slept, and even became a fairground attraction. People used to travel from far and wide and pay money to see him.

Of course, he wasn't human! He was a chicken. The miracle was apparently due to a remarkable series of coincidences. The Olsens, the owners of the farm where Mike lived, chose him for dinner one evening. The mother didn't want to waste the neck, so she aimed to cut it as high as possible. The cut left a good portion of his brain intact, including the part that controlled Mike's heartbeat, breathing and digestion. By another coincidence, a blood clot prevented Mike from bleeding to death. After seeing the headless chicken stand up and run around like when its head was on, the Olsens decided not to eat him for dinner and kept him as a pet. They fed him through the trachea with a dropper, and he continued to grow and fatten after losing his head. Fascinating, maybe, but quite the horror story!

However, your question wasn't about headless chickens but headless humans. Can you imagine a human Mike? Living without a head for a year and a half? Well, no. For a human that would be impossible because when a human body loses its head, it also loses all connection to the brain completely and immediately. And without a connection to the brain, there's no way of running.

It was precisely the immediacy and conclusiveness of death by decapitation that led France to decree the guillotine as the only permitted instrument of execution in 1791. It was chosen for its remarkable efficiency, and for being considered the most humane execution method (causing the least pain and suffering for the person condemned to death) and the least problematic method in front of an audience (decapitations were normally held in public). If those guillotined bodies had started running about the public square, you can bet they would have found a different solution!

If a runner was decapitated halfway through a race, it's possible that inertia might make their body move slightly forwards before collapsing to the ground, but you can be sure they wouldn't reach the finish line!

And what about...
... those fabulously dark stories of guillotined heads making grimaces or even trying to speak? Is it possible? Decapitation immediately cuts off the supply of oxygen, without which the brain cannot work. Even if there was some oxygen left in the blood and tissues after the cut, it wouldn't last long at all. Perhaps there would be some movement of the eyes or the mouth, but they would just be spasms and not conscious movements ordered by the brain. Everything indicates that these tales fit the category of horror stories much better than that of scientific curiosities.

You might also be interested in reading questions 2, 3, 4, and 29.

37. Is there anyone I could ask, please, can I please not die?

Dunia

Dear Dunia,

It doesn't normally make much sense to ask someone for you not to die. Our death (and our life) doesn't normally depend on any one person in particular. There may be some specific cases where it could make sense. For example, if you have someone pointing a gun at you, you could plead for them not to kill you (you could ask them please, can I please, not die?). If you had to undergo a very complicated (life or death) surgical procedure, you could also ask the surgeon to do anything in their hands to save your life (to make sure you don't die). Or if you are in a car with someone driving very fast and you are scared of dying in an accident, you could close your eyes and ask God (if you believe in God) or simply wish out loud (if you are not a believer), not to die. "Please, let me not die today." But in these three cases you wouldn't be asking never to die, but simply not to die at that precise moment in time.

Can you imagine that you could put in a request for immortality? If you could, would you? If the idea appeals to you, you wouldn't be alone. Immortality is one of humanity's oldest desires. Throughout the centuries, we have sought the key to eternal life. For a long time, humans looked to magic as a potential provider of eternal life. Secret potions, sources of water in remote places, mysterious elixirs, sacred chalices, or even miraculous peaches could hold the secret of immortality; and those who managed to find them would triumph over death once and forever. But there is no evidence that anyone ever succeeded.

How about making sure you avoid falling into oblivion?

One way to achieve immortality could be to make sure that you are remembered forever, or at least for many centuries, like the 19th century poet whose poetry we read today, the architect who designed our favorite building, or our great grandmother, whom we remember singing and laughing at family gatherings. They may not be physically alive, but they do "live on," don't they?

What if we requested immortality from a freezer? Yes, people have also fantasized (and still fantasize) with the idea of cryonics: freezing the body of a dead person and keeping it at a very low temperature, until the time in history when science is sufficiently advanced as to be able to revive them and cure them. Can you imagine a 21st century person coming back to life in the 25th century? But the scientific community insists that it is impossible to "wake up" a brain, that it is unlikely to be able to preserve an entire body that way without damaging it, and that there is no indication that a body kept at low temperatures could ever be revived. Still, there are about 500 cryogenically frozen people in the world (and a further 4,000 on the waiting list to join them when they die) waiting for that future, in case it is ever possible.

OK, then. What if we looked to a computer? Virtual immortality! We could scan your brain and transfer it to a computer or another medium. That way, you would not have to worry about your body not being immortal; it would be enough for your mind to be! But this idea raises two important questions: would the result of scanning your brain and transferring it to a digital medium really be your mind? And, even if scanning your brain did allow you to reproduce your mind outside your body, would that mind be you or your digital double?

There's no harm in thinking about the possibilities, of course, but so far, nothing has worked: neither magic, nor ideas about science fiction futures. That is why current science doesn't focus so much on immortality, but rather on aging and the possibilities of prolonging a good life. The kind of good life that might make us ask the surgeon to please, please, save it.

You might also be interested in reading questions 1, 8, and 9.

38. Why do people say "rest in peace" and not "rest in fun"?

Lucía

Dear Lucía,

Your question is full of spark. When you read it, it's almost impossible for your mind not to light up with a party full of dead people having fun. Just picture them! What do you imagine them doing? And what about you? What would you get up to in that eternally fun existence?

Now envision an eternity resting in peace. What exactly do you imagine? Can you think of a way of resting in peace that isn't boring?

But let's get back to your original question, which has two parts. Why do people say "rest in peace"? If you have ever visited a cemetery and looked at the tombstones, you will have often read R. I. P., an abbreviation of the Latin phrase *requiescat in pace*. "Rest in peace" is the translation of those words into English. The phrase was first used in Christian funerals in the 8th century. The inscription *R. I. P.* started to appear regularly on Christian headstones in the 18th century. In Christianity, it is believed that there is an eternal soul, and "rest in peace" is a prayer for the soul of the deceased to find eternal peace in heaven: it is a wish for the soul not to suffer, to be at peace, and to be able to rest.

Did you know that the belief in ghosts comes from the idea that some souls cannot rest in peace? Ghosts would then be, according to that idea, souls in torment, or suffering, wandering souls that cannot reach heaven because they have died with some kind of burden that will not let them rest in peace. So, in a sense, "rest in peace" is a way of saying: "Don't become a ghost!".

Today the phrase "rest in peace" is still widely used, even outside religious contexts. It is used in funerals and burials because it has a solemnity to it that seems appropriate for bidding farewell to a deceased person. We often think of death in those solemn terms. But perhaps it would be nice to think that people we love might rest in fun. As you suggest, why don't we start to say "rest in fun" instead of "rest in peace"? R.I.F!

PS What a great question for the end of this book, Lucía!

You might also be interested in reading questions 14, 18, and 22.

Who made this book?

Concept and Text

ELLEN DUTHIE is a British-Spanish writer, translator and researcher specializing in children's literature and philosophical inquiry with children. Based in Madrid, Spain, she is the cofounder of the publisher Wonder Ponder and the author of the introduction to philosophical curiosity *Is There Anybody Out There?* Her Visual Philosophy for All Ages series won the Andersen Prize for Best Publishing Project in 2023 and her fiction book *Un par de ojos nuevos* won the Spanish Booksellers Association Best Children's Book of the Year in 2022. She has translated books by Maurice Sendak, Jules Feiffer, and John Burningham into Spanish.

ANNA JUAN CANTAVELLA is a social and cultural anthropologist, as well as a specialist in children's literature, based in Barcelona, Spain. She is a visiting lecturer at the University of Barcelona and works as an advisor and researcher in the field of children's literature, designing and teaching courses for both adults and children.

Illustrations

ANDREA ANTINORI is an award-winning Italian illustrator based in Bologna, Italy. He wrote and illustrated the books *The Lives of Lemurs* and *Octopuses Have Zero Bones*. Among many other recognitions, he is the recipient of the International Illustration Prize (Bologna International Children's Book Fair), Best International Illustrated Book (China Shanghai International Children's Book Fair), the Andersen Prize for Best Book 6- to 9-year-olds, and the IBBY Honor List.

Design and Typesetting

STUDIO PATTEN are Aida Novoa and Carlos Egan, illustrators and designers.

Expert Review

XAVIERA TORRES is a biologist specializing in the history of science. She works in the fields of science outreach and cultural mediation. She is the coauthor of the science podcast for kids, *La lupa sónica*, and also writes children's books.

MONTSE COLILLES CODINA lives and works in Barcelona as a child psychologist, early childhood education advisor, and children's literature specialist.

The authors want to give...
... a very warm thank you to all those adults out there who embraced the idea of chatting with kids about death and took the time and effort to collect and send us the questions that arose from those conversations. And we want to give a very special thanks to all those mortals aged 5 to 15 whose questions are at the very heart of this book.

DYING TO ASK
THUMP THUMP
WAS CONCEIVED
THUMP THUMP
WRITTEN
THUMP THUMP
ILLUSTRATED
THUMP THUMP
TRANSLATED
THUMP THUMP
DESIGNED
THUMP THUMP
TYPESET
THUMP THUMP
EDITED
THUMP THUMP
PROOFREAD
THUMP THUMP
PRINTED
THUMP THUMP
DISTRIBUTED
THUMP THUMP
AND SOLD
THUMP THUMP
BY LIVING HUMAN BEINGS.
HAVE YOU READ IT YET?
THUMP THUMP

Dying to Ask: 38 Questions from Kids About Death was first published in the United States by Tra Publishing in 2024
Text by Ellen Duthie © 2023 & Anna Juan Cantavella © 2023
Illustrations by Andrea Antinori © 2023
Graphic design by Studio Patten
Translated by Ellen Duthie © 2024
Translation rights arranged by Agencia Literaria CBQ

Original edition: Wonder Ponder / Traje de lobo S.L.
Original title: *¿Así es la muerte?: 38 preguntas mortales de niños y niñas*

U.S. Edition
Publisher & Creative Director
Ilona Oppenheim

Art Director/Cover Design
Jefferson Quintana

Designer/Typesetter
Leonardo van Schermbeek

Editorial Director
Lisa McGuinness

Publishing Coordinator
Jessica Faroy

Printed and bound in China by
Shenzhen Reliance Printers

This book is printed on Forest Stewardship Council-certified paper from well-managed forests. Tra Publishing is committed to sustainability in its materials and practices.

MIX
Paper from
responsible sources
FSC® C102842

ISBN: 978-1-962098-06-9

Tra Publishing
245 NE 37th Street
Miami, FL 33137
trapublishing.com

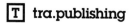

1 2 3 4 5 6 7 8 9 10

• Is death one dream after another? (Fernando, 10) • Can you change your clothes when you die (from the clothes you were wearing when you died)? (Heiðný, 5) • When you are dead, is it a whole other life that never ends? (Gael, 8) • When we die, do we become ghosts? (Andrea, 10) • Can you die from wearing a mask? (Anonymous, 9) • How can a cat die? (Heiðný, 5) • How does the spirit reach heaven? (Héctor, 10) • Does death have a physical appearance? (Amanda, 10) • Why does death exist? (Jacob, 10) • When you die, can someone snatch your body before you are buried? (Anonymous, 9) • If you suffer from claustrophobia, how can you stand it inside a coffin? (Florrie, 11) • When we die, does all our body die suddenly? (Anonymous, 9) • What is there after death? (Hugo, 13; Estela, 10; Manu, 10; Uma, 12) • If you died, would you want to come back to life? (Pamela, 12) • Can we reincarnate? Or go on to an afterlife? (Bryan, 11) • When you are dead, do you have blood? (Anonymous, 8) • Can it be your birthday in heaven? (Anonymous, 8) • Is death real? (Mariana, 8) • When I die, will I remember? (Sira, 6) • Why does death arrive earlier for some people than for others? (Nerea, 10) • When we die, do we meet up with our relatives who are no longer alive? (Unai, 10) • What happens with our soul? (Eloi, 10) • Why don't they give people an injection to help them die when they are sick, like they do with animals? (Marc, 8) • If you eat a pizza and you choke to death, what happens to the pizza? Does it stay in your body? (Anonymous, 9) • Why do we die? (Ángel, 8) • When we die, does our heart stop? (Dasha, 8) • Why do some people donate their organs when they die? (Nataly, 8) • When you die, do you go to heaven, to hell, or do you stay in your grave? (Anonymous, 9) • Is there a life after death? (Mariama, 8 and Uma, 12) • When you dream, are you dead or alive? (Mijael, 8) • When we die, do we see a tunnel with light at the end of it? (Islam, 8) • Why do we cry when someone dies? (Marc, 8) • Why do we see God when we die? (Mariama, 8) • Why do we bury the dead? (Ángel, 8) • Can you dance if you are dead? (Anonymous, 9) • Do we keep growing when we are dead? (Ariba, 8) • Do we celebrate birthdays when we are dead? (Raquel, 8) • Why do worms eat you when you die? (Emmanuel, 8) • Do we have feelings after we die? (Nataly, 8) • If we die, do we remember? (Marc, 8) • If we die, are we born again? (Sora, 8) • What does it feel like to be dead? (Anonymous, 9) • What would you like to do before you die? (Fernanda, 8, and Alejandro, 12) • When someone dies, do we all react the same way? (Nerea, 9) • What does it feel like to be poisoned? (Fernando, 8) • If it is true that there are spirits, do they wear any clothes? (Fernanda, 9) • When we die, does our soul go up to heaven or does it stay around for a while in the place where we die? (Gadiel, 9) • Are ghosts invisible? Is there anywhere we can store them away? (Daniel, 9) • What age can we live to? (Anonymous, 10) • Why do dead bodies stink? (Meylin, 9) • When you die, do you suffer? (Marc, 8) • How long does a skeleton last? (Gael, 8) • When we die, why do our eyes stay open? (Mishal, 9) • After we die, what do they do with the clothes we are wearing? (Ismael, 9) • Why do they dress the dead in white in India and Pakistan? (Afiya, 9) • If we die, are we then born again as children? (Gadiel, 9) • If we behave badly, when we die, are we sent to hell and burned? (Verónica, 9) • What happens to our hair when we die? (Ismael, 9) • A question for a vampire—what would you do if you were dead? (María Cecilia, 9) • Do the dead play among themselves? (Daniel, 9) • If you are in heaven, how is it possible that you are also in your grave? (Anonymous, 9) • Why do people say "rest in peace" and not "rest in fun"? (Lucía, 9) • Is death the end or the beginning of everything? (Nagore, 11) • Do the dead sleep? (Gadiel, 9) • In heaven, is there a world like this one but full of spirits? (Héctor, 10) · Where does our body's blood go when we die? (Mishal, 9) · Why do they dress up dead bodies and make them look nice if they are going to be buried afterwards? (Arthur, 9) · If you are not a Christian, will you go to hell? (Anonymous, 9) · Why aren't children allowed to see the dead? (Fernanda, 9) · Would you rather die with someone by your side or alone? (Marina, 11) · Why do we give flowers to the dead if they cannot take them? (Meylin, 9) · Are we living or just dying slowly? (Uzinga, 11) · If you die, does your spirit stay alive? (Juliana, 11) · Does it hurt when you die? (Gia, 11) · If you are immortal and you jump out of a window, do you get injured? Does it hurt? (Anonymous, 9) · How long does it take for a corpse to decompose? (Mikaela, 10) · Is death scary? (Christian, 11, and Leire, 11) · Where does our soul go when we die? (Mikaela, 10) · If we are cremated, does our soul survive? (Maily, 10) · What would happen if they buried me alive? (Paula, 10) · What do you feel when you die? (Izan, 10) · A question for a skeleton— what does it feel like not to have any flesh or skin? (Florrie, 11) · When you are dead, are you a god? (Anonymous, 9) · What does it feel like when you die? (Nabil, 11) · How long would it take for your body to decompose in space? (Núria, 11) · Where do you go when you die? (Marco, 11) · When you are dead, do you eat? (Anonymous, 9) · When will they invent a time machine to know when you will die? (Yuma, 11) · When you are dead, is it scary? (Maria, 12) · What's the meaning of life if we are going to die? (Luz Mary, 13) · Why do we hold funerals when people die? (Gia, 11) · Could I be a ghost? (Jóhann, 12) · Is it possible to become a ghost? (Anonymous, 8) · Can you move when you are dead? (Heiðný, 5) · Do you think that what you do in life will affect you when you are dead? (Marcos, 15) · Is there any fate worse than death? (Ali, 9, and Gael, 8) · If you are dead, can you remember your parents, your brothers and sisters, and your friends? (Zian, 5) · Can you have a heart and a brain when you are dead? (Dunia, 5) · When you are dead, does anything hurt? (Sifdin, 5) · When you die, are you born again in the body of a newborn without knowing that you have lived in another body before? (Elma, 11) · Is it sad to bury someone? (Julia, 5) · What do you feel before you die? (Enma, 11) · Can we open our eyes and speak to Jesus when we are dead? (Anonymous, 5) · If you are dead, can you leave your grave? (Abel, 5) · How does skin go away? (Nacho, 5) · After dying, do you come back to life in a different body? (Anna, 10) · How do you become a skeleton? (Iván, 5) · When you die, do you become a ghost? (Valentina, 11) · How do you become a ghost? (Julen, 5) · When you die, do you have any hair? (Carla, 5) · If you are dead, can you see and hear living people? (Fernando, 5) · Do you suffer if, when you are dead, a vampire sucks your blood? (César, 5) · If I die making a silly face, will it stay like that forever? (Anonymous, 7) · Would you rather be alive or dead? (Sofía, 5) · What happens in our body and in our soul when we die? (Lara, 12) · What do you feel when you are dead? (Mikaela, 10) · How do they put you in the grave? (Acher, 5) · When you die, does your angry spirit come out? (Clàudia, 5) · When I go to sleep, how do I know that I haven't died? (Zian, 8, and Mijael, 8) · When you die, do you dream? (Valentina, 11) · Do people who you love very much stay with you even after they die? (Anonymous, 6) · Is it bad luck to die? (Jóhann, 12) · Why do we die forever? (Luca, 8) · When you die is it only your body that dies and not your soul? (Lara, 12) · And what is Grandpa going to do in there all day, inside the coffin? (Jan, 8) · What thoughts cross your mind when you are about to die, and you know it? (Marina, 11) · When you are dead, can you dream? (Leire, 11) · How long can humans live for? (Maily, 10) · When you die, do you